Setting up home

Nicholas Hills and
Barty Phillips

a Design Centre book
published by Quick Fox

Setting up home
First edition published 1978
A Design Centre book published
in the United Kingdom by
Design Council 28 Haymarket
London SW1Y 4SU

Designed by Anne Fisher
Printed and bound in the United
Kingdom by Balding+Mansell Ltd,
London and Wisbech

Distributed throughout the continents
of North America, including Canada,
and South America by Quick Fox,
33 West 60th Street, New York,
NY 10023

International Standard Book Number 0-8256-3124-6
Library of Congress Catalog Card Number 78-51867

Contents

Introduction

A first home often just evolves; you don't give yourself the chance to plan it. By the time you've found the right property, arranged a mortgage, paid the conveyancing fees and realised how much the rates are, you feel it's a miracle that you're moving in at all; planning, you feel, is something that will have to wait. This should not be so; there are many ways in which forward planning will help you later on.

This book discusses the necessity of knowing yourself before planning for your needs, with an eye to the economy invariably necessary when considering a first home. It is about the space you call home, and about the flexibility and adaptability of the arrangements within that space.

Flexibility implies that you can carry on more than one function in a space, a simple example being when a room is used for both living and sleeping. Adaptability suggests that the original arrangement, whether of walls or a furniture grouping, can be readily and conveniently altered as your needs change. This suggests a rather abstract assessment of your possible needs from the beginning, and it is very often true that you only find out what you really need as time goes on. However, don't ignore this line of thought, as how you begin invariably becomes a fixed pattern for life, and this pattern will affect your physical and even intellectual comfort.

An ingenious and attractive solution to sleeping in a multi-purpose room. The wooden bed structure forms a canopy over the sofa. In such an arrangement there must be sufficient headroom at both levels.
Designer: Derek Frost

MICHAEL NICHOLSON/ELIZABETH WHITING

The grand plan

Choosing a home

If you are working there are many reasons why you should live as near where you work as possible. You would do well to find out how easy it is to get to the station by public transport; how frequently the trains run; how much a monthly season ticket would cost and how much the local station charges for parking a car.

Find out about local amenities, for both yourself and other members of your family. Check whether there's a public library, cinema, golf course or tennis club. You may want to take part in local activities such as the Women's Institute, Townswomen's Guild or Gingerbread group, and you will need a reasonable public transport service to make this possible. If you have a mother's help or lodger, he or she will need the same facilities and want a chance to meet friends. A bored and lonely person will leave as soon as the chance arises.

If there's a garden make sure it's not blighted by aircraft noise or lack of sun. Very often, if you are looking around at a weekend, the area may seem quiet and peaceful and only on a weekday will you realise that there's a noisy factory or a playground on the other side of the wall.

In 1961 a committee headed by Sir Parker Morris drew up a series of recommendations for minimum building standards in council housing, called *Homes for Today and Tomorrow*. They have been used since then by architects and local authority builders as acceptable basic requirements for all dwellings. Houses built before that time may not all have been brought up to this standard, but when converted should have certain basic amenities such as a kitchen with hot and cold water, a bathroom, adequate 13 amp power points, and suitable ventilation; there is also a recommendation as to minimum room sizes.

The recommendations also covered space for prams and bicycles downstairs, so if your house was not built to the Parker Morris standards, and you have or are likely to need a pram or a bicycle, see if there's space for one. Also check whether there's room for an extra lavatory; when the basic planning is at fault, it is sometimes difficult to find a cure apart from reconstruction.

Many first homes are founded in those parts of houses that are not much sought after, such as basements and attics. The view out of a basement is invariably limited to the basement area, although the light can be practically as good as on the ground floor of a house. If you are converting a basement yourself, there are rules governing the size of a room in relation to the amount of light entering. Briefly: light angles are drawn at 30 degrees to the horizontal through the head and sill of the window. The area of light measured between these two lines, multiplied by the width of the window, should be no less than one tenth of the floor area. If you are not going to employ your own architect, the local planning officer may be able to help you to work out this fundamentally important aspect of forming a home below ground level.

One advantage of living in a basement flat is that it often has a garden. If not, you can very easily make one with bags of soil and compost. But take care not to heap up top soil against the walls of the house, because this can conduct water up the brickwork and into the building.

A flat in an attic can be enormous fun. On the one hand you have the possibility of exploiting the attractive internal construction, and on the other you have an opportunity to raise the existing roof and fit larger windows which will provide glorious views and as much sunlight as you want. Here again, design is important, this time from the town planning point of view.

Too often one sees buildings with a jumbly accretion of rooftop additions. Setting back new dormer windows from the face of a building is invariably desirable, except perhaps when they are designed in the traditional form of small windows set into a mansard roof. There is the advantage also that a roof terrace, or even a roof garden, can be created in front of the new windows. When converting an attic, remember to insulate it adequately first (see page 10).

Don't be put off by dull or depressing decorations and poor decorative condition. It is very easy to transform a house yourself with time and paint, and redecorating from scratch helps fulfil the basic instinct most of us have for modifying our environment.

new dormer window

former roof light

2.3m

4.5m

Above: This cross-section through an attic room shows how the roof space can be enlarged to increase the usable floor area by inserting a dormer window at one side. The height of an attic room must be not less than 2·3m over an area of at least half of the room, measured at 1m from the floor.

Below: This cross-section through a basement room shows the minimum requirements permitted for a habitable room. The window area must be not less than one-tenth of the area of the room, the part calculated being within a zone angled at 30 degrees to the horizontal.

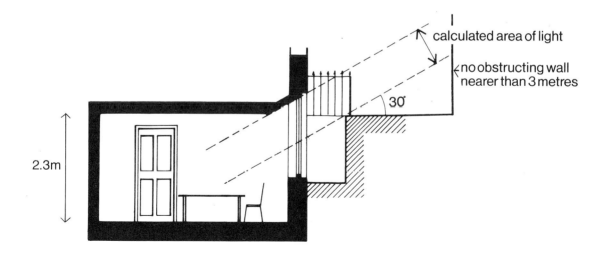

calculated area of light

no obstructing wall nearer than 3 metres

30°

2.3m

Planning

Part of the planning operation is to get the work sequence right. If you are hoping to have the house rewired as soon as you can afford it in, say, a year's time, you can decide not to do any serious redecorating until the wiring has been done—otherwise you would have to do it all over again at great cost and waste of time. When thinking ahead, study the wiring and socket outlets you will need and seek advice from your local Electricity Board showroom.

There's one exception to this rule. However ambitious or far ahead your plans, do decorate one room straight away and have it as you mean to. Then, no matter how gloomy the rest of the house, no matter how impractical it is or how dirty the workmen or how beastly the rebuilding and how tiresome, you have one place you can retreat to which is really comfortable, really cosy and above all, really yours.

Other kinds of planning are equally helpful and money saving. For instance, leaving spaces in the kitchen for major appliances which you can't yet afford but know you will want to buy later; or designing a children's room with furniture that is not too big or grand for a baby but that can be adapted as the children grow older without your having to buy expensive new things.

You can provide spaces for what you plan to buy and fill them with something else in the meantime. In the kitchen, you can fit a worktop which will eventually cover all the machinery such as a dishwasher, small food freezer and washing machine and fill the present gaps with whitewood furniture or shelves, slotting the new appliances under the worktop as and when you get them. In children's rooms shelving systems are often better than tables and bookcases, and the kind of cot that extends later into a bed may be cheaper in the long run than a progression of cribs, cots and beds.

A family is a living, moving, changing unit, and circumstances change in unexpected ways, so you must try to think about all the probabilities and adopt a flexible approach at each stage.

Consider the implications of children, who will grow older, bigger and more independent; of looking after an elderly relative; and whether you will need extra washing and cooking facilities later on. Finally, every house needs its 'den'; somewhere for romping, working, train sets or what you will.

The kitchen reduced to its simplest terms: white plastics laminate facing to cabinets and stainless steel worktops. Note the spaces left for additional appliances. The table is placed at the window end of the room, where it will not get in the way of people walking in and out; it also takes advantage of the view of the garden.
Architect: Yorke Rosenberg Mardall

Heating

Before you get down to details you should decide what sort of heating you want. A warm house is a friendly house, but take care not to fall for any of the cheap-sounding central heating installations that you may see advertised. They may be cheap to buy, but are often fearfully expensive to run. If you are installing a heating system but have only limited funds, have the boiler designed to cope with full central heating even if you install only part initially.

If you live in a town, a gas-fired boiler will be the best economy, especially as you may not have room for an oil storage tank. In the country, where there may not be a gas supply, the most convenient fuels are oil and bottled gas.

Electricity can be supplied at a cheap rate if used at certain non-peak times of the day, and this is particularly helpful if you have night storage heaters. Ask for details at your local Electricity Board showroom, and make sure you specify which tariff you want to be charged on once the appliance has been installed.

For a small flat with few rooms, a solid-fuel back boiler, which burns anthracite or the smokeless fuel required in urban areas, can be very economical. Not only can you heat your main room, but the water and a couple of radiators too. During the summer, of course, you may want to use an immersion heater which can be connected to a time switch to provide hot water only when you need it.

There is a large variety of solid-fuel stoves, usually with doors in the front, which burn anything from coke to peat, wood and even dung. They can provide year-round hot water, because you can close the doors during the summer when you do not need the radiant heat. The appearance of these is often more appropriate in a modern or informal setting, and three good looking models are illustrated here.

There are stoves that will do the cooking and heat water for a family of four. These again can burn oil, gas or solid fuel. They act as very effective radiators in the kitchen, though you may find them too hot in the summer and prefer to use an immersion heater for the hot water and a baby stove to cook on.

You must also decide at this stage what type of radiator you want and where they are to be installed. The flat, narrow sort usually looks better than fat, ribbed ones, though under a window a fat one can look quite jolly and you can even sit on it.

Above right: The tiny Bijou traditional French stove can be used for simple cooking. Below: This sleek cast iron stove clad in stainless steel is available with a back boiler

for hot water. Made by Pither Below right: The traditional French Godin stove will burn several types of solid fuel. The steel body has enamel decoration.

Insulation

You can save enormous sums on your heating bills if you insulate your house really effectively. Another advantage is that insulation reduces condensation appreciably, which in turn means that you should have less deterioration of paint and wallcoverings, so long-term redecorating costs will be lower too.

There are three main ways in which you can insulate.

Roofs

Since 1975 most houses have been built with a 50mm blanket of insulation in the roof space to meet the minimum requirement of the Building Regulations. However, even this is not really effective and about 80 per cent of houses built before that have no insulation at all. It is now generally accepted that a depth of 75mm is satisfactory, and 100mm preferable.

You can use glass fibre or spun mineral wool mat or quilt bought in rolls, which is proofed against damp, vermin, fire and rot. Reflective aluminium foil can also be used; it is cheap but less effective than other materials. You can use insulating board, or you can 'loose fill' the spaces between the joists with cork, vermiculite or polystyrene granules, or mineral wool, glass wool or glass fibre pellets.

Walls

On the whole, more heat is lost through walls than through any other part of a house, unless you live in a bungalow where there's a comparatively large roof area; in this case you will possibly lose more through the roof.

Your home may have cavity walls or solid walls. Cavity wall insulation involves the injection of foam or mineral wool into the cavity. This must be undertaken by a reputable specialist. If you decide to use a local firm, ask the advice of your local council as to which firms they can recommend or ask a reputable local builder. It's extremely important to get this job done properly. You can often tell whether you've got a cavity or a solid wall by measuring its thickness: 280mm is probably cavity; 225mm solid.

Draughtproofing

Draughts are the cause of something like 20 per cent of heat losses from most homes. They get in through doors and window frames; through fireplaces; cracks in the walls; gaps in floorboards and skirtings; letter boxes; outlet pipes or through the eaves where the joists meet the roof.

You can get several types of draught excluder to stick or tack onto the bottom of doors, or fix round the door jamb and window frames. Failing this, masking tape stuck round windows that you don't need to open in winter will keep out draughts; you can pull it off in summer without tearing off the paint as well.

Condensation

Condensation can cause a host of problems within the house, from damage to decorations through mildew; peeling wall and ceiling paper; flaking paint on window frames; and a musty smell. Condensation often seems insidious. It is likely for example that many of the instances of water penetration in new largely concrete flats are caused by water vapour condensing on the cold inner face of external walls.

The condensation of water vapour held in suspension in the air is generally caused by a combination of three factors: insufficient heat, insufficient insulation and insufficient ventilation.

To prevent condensation all three must be avoided to a certain extent, but the prime necessities are insulation and heat, for without a cold surface in the room the water vapour in the air cannot condense.

The problem is often serious in bathrooms, especially after somebody has taken a bath or shower. A ducted air extractor fan is essential in an internal bathroom (which has no window), and a useful addition even where there is a window. However, please do not fit it into the glass, as this looks ugly from both inside and out. In an internal bathroom the extractor fan must be connected to the light switch with a 20-minute overrun and with a standby motor in case of failure.

The bedroom is a place where condensation is often most bothersome. Most people like a bedroom rather cool as a dry warm atmosphere dries the throat. Always maintain a small amount of cross ventilation by leaving a door slightly ajar and a fanlight just open. In winter you may need to keep on a small $\frac{1}{2}$kw heater if your central heating goes off on a time switch. This should ensure some convection current which can carry away the water vapour.

Kitchens (like bathrooms) are well known for their condensation problems. Here really good ventilation is desirable in order to carry away cooking smells as well as water vapour and not let them waft into the rest of the house. Always try to afford an extractor hood over a cooker. This can even be a home-made affair with a fan set in a box with a 150mm to 200mm diameter flexible pipe extended to the outside air.

A very helpful leaflet called *Condensation* (No. 61) is available from HMSO. It explains more fully the other problems you may face and how you could deal with them.

Sound insulation
Tolerance to sound varies from person to person. One needs to try to create a condition where unwanted sounds are diminished as much as possible and wanted sounds, such as music, are heard at their best.

Carpets, curtains and textured wallcoverings all help to reduce noise. When there are only one or two people in a house noise may not seem much of a problem, but several people may generate a disturbing build-up of noise. Then is the time to consider laying some sort of tough carpet or carpet tiles, especially in upstairs rooms or in an open-plan space.

Families in North America and Scandinavia, who design children into their lives, often have a basement area for their teenagers where they can make as much noise as they like without imposing on other members of the household. Acoustic ceilings can help with sound. Too many hard surfaces will cause both pleasant and unpleasant noises to bounce backwards and forwards like ping pong balls, so a balance of hard and soft is necessary.

Advice

There are many sources of help on all aspects of planning a home. There is a comprehensive list on page 71, and you will find helpful addresses in your local Yellow Pages.

The Building Centre in London has exhibitions of various building materials and heating techniques, an enquiry desk where you can get information on specialist firms and materials as well as a comprehensive bookshop.

The Design Centres in London and Glasgow mount permanent displays of well designed modern British consumer goods. You can consult Design Index, in which products of all kinds considered to be of good design are photographed and listed with approximate prices and manufacturers' addresses. In the London Design Centre further help is available at an information desk, and there is a well stocked bookshop.

Your local planning office will help in many respects if you want to find out about whether there are regulations on new plumbing you plan to do; on extensions; knocking down walls; basement flats and so on.

No matter how well you think you know yourself, you may find that a professional can see things about you that you don't see yourself. If you decide to seek professional advice on setting up a new home the best time to do this is obviously before you have settled on a particular property. Even as a dispassionate observer, an architect or designer who concentrates on housing design will be able to advise you on the sort of property that could

best suit you and moreover he can see the potential possibilities in even semi-derelict buildings which you might not.

Even if you are adapting a typical suburban semi for your own needs, let your architect explain with sketches and perspective drawings what he is trying to do; you will soon develop a professional eye for interpreting such drawings. And debate with him the pros and cons of this or that arrangement, especially in the bathroom and kitchen but also in the basic planning of the rest of the house. It is important to find an architect whose work you feel sympathetic towards and who is used to dealing with housing. Any self-respecting architect will feel it necessary to get to know his client and his way of life before deciding on a suitable plan. (Advice on choosing an architect or designer is on page 63.)

Know thyself- and thy family

What is your life? From all the planning and design possibilities, how can you decide what is best to do unless you have first decided what sort of person you are and what sort of life you want to lead? In this chapter we look at the important things you should be asking yourself. It's not just a question of decorative style; it's more a question of the sort of life you lead, and that should be the prime factor in deciding how your house is kitted out.

Planning your new home may mean the opportunity to start from the beginning with everything – husband or wife, bed, kitchen, even new friends. Or you may be going to carry on an established routine but in different surroundings. You will want your home to be part of your way of life – but which way of life? Do you want to work at home or do you want home to be a haven from a busy working life outside? Do you want to be the centre of a large family or lead a quiet, uninterrupted existence?

You may be arriving at your new home after living in temporary accommodation or staying with parents or parents-in-law for several weeks, months or even years, during which time you may have developed a fixed image of what you want – and more particularly what you do not want your new home to be like.

Individuality

Whatever else your home does, it must allow you to live and behave as best suits you. It's no good creating a *House and Garden* showpiece if you are in fact a happy-go-lucky slut at heart and your work and interests create their own disorder. If you are a gregarious person you certainly won't be happy in a house that is a series of little rooms shut off from each other. This is especially true of the kitchen, where many people feel dreadfully imprisoned as they slave away in a cell-like space while family and friends are whooping it up at the far end of a passage.

Planning for one has its problems, but planning for two may bring to light all sorts of differences in temperament and taste you never knew existed. Single people often have a fairly definite idea of how they want to live. For couples or families it's altogether more complicated, and a failure to understand this may lead to a lot of frustration and irritation. For one person a showpiece living room may be very important, for another a well equipped study. One may think that the bedroom should be a haven of floral bliss, another that it could and should be a useful working room for sewing or typing or even an extra living room with a second television set. In fact, almost everyone really needs a room, however tiny, he can get away to.

Plan your home to include for everybody's quirks. If there are fights about what to watch on television, consider getting another set. They're not expensive to rent and in any case it's a small price to pay for peace.

Some like it hot, some like it cold. We've known couples who have waged constant internal warfare about central heating. You may have to compromise between 15°C and 20°C, but it is important that everybody feels warm enough in the house.

If there's one very tall and one very short person in the house, someone will have to decide what size the bath should be. (Perhaps a bit of vertical thinking could solve the problem by deciding on the height of a shower fitting instead.)

Families

It is not until you have small children that you realise how enormously they will change your life. Most parents have to learn to live with children's grubby fingermarks, crumby carpets, jammy smears and scuffed skirtings. So if you have children try to make sure all your finishes are tough, washable and dirt concealing and all your furniture sturdy and reliable. It would be inappropriate, for example, to have flock wallpaper on the staircase (even if your tastes tend in this direction) if you have three small boys rushing up and down stairs all day. If you want to romp on the carpet with your children or play boisterous games, there is no point having a room crowded with expensive china on fragile tables.

A problem which besets families is coping with the needs of growing children. When children are young they may be obstreperous but you have them more or less under your control. Eventually blessed bedtime will arrive and they can be put away and you have the house to yourselves. But do bear in mind that your children will grow older and will need space in which to develop and spread themselves. Eventually, an attic or even a garden shed may be a blessing if you can find the space and make it habitable.

Others in the house

The whole subject of others in the house is worth thinking about at the early planning stage. There are many reasons why you might want to incorporate into your household people from outside your immediate family. For instance, you may need someone to help in the home for a time; you may simply need the cash a lodger can offer; or you may want to make a home for a relative or a friend from abroad.

Almost always it is best to make this accommodation as self contained as you possibly can. In fact, we think it is often a good idea to have every bedroom in the house almost self contained – rather like study bedrooms in a university college where at least you can boil an egg and entertain a friend without everybody in the house having to know all about it. Everyone needs a certain amount of privacy at certain times; you can't live separately in any sense from those who must share your front door, your lavatory, your kitchen and even your television set. These things apply to everybody, whether family or outsiders.

Specific requirements

Although it is convenient to categorise people, no one person has exactly the same requirements as another. So it's impossible to establish exact rules for setting up home, but the following list may help to ensure that you are asking yourself the right questions:

1 How many rooms will you want to use as bedrooms? Are they in use all the time?
2 How many meals will you want to prepare each day and for how many people? This may determine kitchen size, disposition and layout and whether you need to incorporate a special dining area in the kitchen. (It is less convenient to have to lay three meals a day in a separate room and involves more work.)

In this spacious kitchen cum family room, the mother can keep an eye on her small daughter while she is cooking. Sealed cork tiles provide a practical flooring.

TOM BIRO

3 Do you need to entertain friends or business colleagues to dinner? (This may determine whether you need a separate dining room.) Many people are content to eat and entertain in a reasonably sophisticated way in a carefully designed kitchen.

4 Do you need a room where someone can play a musical instrument? This will definitely need a separate room for everyone's sake. There may be other noisy or space-using activities, such as play readings, discussion groups and coffee mornings, which all need space, seating and uncluttered rooms. If you have only one living room you may decide to put the television set in a bedroom – your own perhaps.

5 Have you got a plan of all your activities and interests? Try to see that there's available space for everything you want to do.

This simple self-questioning means that you should be able to decide more easily and effectively how to make the best use of available space rather than just furnish rooms as they come.

Layout of individual rooms

As you go round your new house assessing your past experiences and your present and possible future needs, don't accept the present layout of the house necessarily as inevitable. Spaces can often be changed, rooms given a new function and it needn't always be expensive. Here are some suggestions:

Kitchen

Your kitchen is likely to pose some of the worst problems and demand the most exacting decisions. Even if you don't do a lot of exotic cooking, you will probably find you spend a good deal of time in the kitchen, so you must make sure it's a room you can enjoy and in which you can work comfortably and efficiently. It should be easy to clean, good to look at, friendly, warm and – even if you like small kitchens – you should at least be able to swing a cat in it. If you're a person who likes company or if you want to keep an eye on a young family, your kitchen should be spacious, with room for toys and games, a good sized table and the chairs to go round it, and at least one chair you can relax in.

Many kitchens are pretty small. This might be acceptable to people who like to cook in a compact space, but only if you can give it the efficiency and organisation of a ship's galley. If you can't you should really consider knocking down a wall to make a larger kitchen/dining room or even moving lock stock and barrel to another more convenient room altogether. This will be an expensive move and may mean you will have to get a larger mortgage or put off buying an expensive carpet or a modern cooker or even both for a year or two, but in terms of contentment it could be worth waiting.

Alternatively you might be able to add a small home extension; it would take up a small piece of the garden but

might at the same time give you a better outlook and a more convenient way out to pick herbs.

Whatever your attitude to cooking there are certain basic things to look out for in the kitchen:

First, for convenience' sake, cooker, sink and food storage should be fairly close to each other and certainly not on opposite walls of a large kitchen or you'll constantly be padding backwards and forwards. It is useful to have a working surface between them. If there simply isn't room you should try at least to have one worktop big enough for measuring, chopping, mixing, rolling pastry and all the paraphernalia that goes with these operations. If you have room for a kitchen table, so much the better. For safety's sake, don't have the cooker next to a door or under a window. It's much better for everyone if the kitchen doesn't have to be used as a passage between house and garden.

There should be plenty of room to store fresh, dried and tinned food; draining plates; saucepans and lids (near the cooker); bottles, jars and cookery books; also space for sitting down when you shell peas or peel potatoes. Wall cupboards should not be fixed where the doors will hit your head when open, and there should be plenty of room to open doors of appliances so they don't knock into other appliances or walls. There should also be plenty of room to bend down to get things out of the oven.

Don't ignore your own individual requirements: whether you like lots of space or a small room; whether you are single or cook for a large family; sociable or a loner; what type of food you like to cook; whether you would like it to be your office as well; and whether you will do your laundry there.

The kitchen is not the best place for laundry, since clothes and especially dirty clothes don't really mix with cooking, but there may be no alternative for a large family with no nearby launderette and a bathroom that is too small for washing clothes. If you do have to do the washing in the kitchen you will need more space: space for a washing machine and possibly a tumbler drier and a clothes rack of some kind; space for sorting and storing the laundry; and perhaps also space for doing the ironing.

Elderly people, however, who may move slowly and have lost some of the strength in their fingers and find stretching and stooping difficult, will welcome smaller kitchens and convenient storage – not too high and not too low.

Living room

If you use the living room mainly for reading and watching television, you probably won't need a big one. But if the room is likely to be needed for several activities, such as eating, playing cards or other table games, sewing, even parties and dancing, you will need a large space to house the extra furniture required. You will also need good lighting and some fairly efficient sound-deadening materials, such as carpet, cork and woolly fabrics.

If the present living room is down-stairs, a bit dark and pokey, and overlooks a boring street, why not move it upstairs? With luck you'll get a better view, it will be less noisy and perhaps more spacious.

Conversation is the main activity in most living rooms, and planning and designing a room for this function can be as exacting as designing a workable bathroom. People often talk in pairs, so the grouping of sofas or chairs should be planned with this in mind.

The living room is the one room in the house that reflects your cultural interests most. Curiously, there are still people who – even with limited space – use it for formal entertaining only, and spend most of the time uncomfortably in a cramped kitchen corner or

elsewhere, not wanting to 'wear out' the good sofas and carpets. This attitude is as nihilistic in its way as the other extreme, where greasy-backed armchairs with sagging upholstery, unemptied ashtrays and wobbly legged tables are strewn around the television set, like a lounge in a seedy hotel.

There should be a balance. Remember, the room is primarily for your use, and just as you dress with reasonable tidiness, not to say style and elegance, you should dress your room as a further extension of your personality and taste. You will get a sense of spiritual well-being in a room that is pleasantly lit, warm and comfortable.

Bedroom

Don't automatically take the biggest room as your own bedroom. If you don't intend to work or read in it or spend other than sleeping time there, why not let the children have it? It might even encourage them to spend more time there and less messing up the kitchen. It is generally quieter at the back of a house, so bear this in mind when allocating bedrooms.

You might find it useful to buy a sofa bed, bunk beds, or beds that fold up against a wall or into a cupboard unit, or you can have inflatable mattresses, roll-up camping beds, foam seating, a divan or foam mattress cushions, which can be used by visitors.

Children's room

If you want to encourage your children (or mother's help or lodger) to spend time in their own room, you must make the room worth spending time in. The size doesn't matter too much if the room has a pleasant outlook, nice big window and a workable shape, though the bigger it is the more scope it offers for variety; universities and colleges looking for rooms to recommend to students specify a certain size. Children need space to expand and play, build bricks, set up railways, spread their belongings around and later do homework and display models or dolls. If you don't provide a warm and happy atmosphere for them they'll choose to work and play elsewhere – in the kitchen or living room – or give up and prefer not to be at home at all.

Bathroom/lavatory

Many houses are cursed with very tiny bathrooms which are often pokey, cold and unpleasant; where two or more people can't wash at the same time; and in which it is not possible to fit laundry facilities. A bathroom is much more suitable than a kitchen for doing the laundry, provided the equipment is properly installed.

When looking at a house, and particularly with a view to an expanding household, you should see whether there'll be an opportunity to have a second bathroom or lavatory. A small

third bedroom can usefully be converted into a bathroom, perhaps en suite with the main bedroom.

To save both hot water and space, you might like to consider installing a shower instead of a bath. This would save you a good deal of money if you were thinking of moving house anyway when you can afford to. If the bathroom is very tiny you could put in a very small bath – the modern version of a sitz bath. There is a small, square plastics one with a built-in seat which you sit up in. This type can even be built in under the stairs, serving the main bedroom or the children's, mother's help's or lodger's room. They are also very convenient for the elderly.

Below left: Sealed cork tiles cover all the surfaces in this minimally planned bathroom, and the mirror fixed along the entire length of one wall creates an illusion of increased space.
Below: To cater for the needs of a large family, one bathroom was converted into two. The inner bathroom shown here has no natural daylight, so borrowed light from the outer bathroom is provided by a double-glazed 'porthole'; the room is artificially ventilated. The floor-to-ceiling mirror covers an old corner chimney breast.

JERRY TUBBY/ELIZABETH WHITING

Workroom

Nearly every home needs a workroom of some kind, whether it's for serious hobbies or for the efficient running of the house – for dealing with bills, telephone calls, paperwork, filing and so on. Sometimes a corner of the living room or kitchen is room enough, or you may prefer to set aside a room specially for the activity. A small, odd-shaped room may be just right for someone's hobby and it certainly won't do any harm to make it double as a spare bedroom for short-term stays. A little room can make a perfectly convenient darkroom or workroom for sewing and crafts, where concentrated storage for materials and tools is useful.

Hall

A hall must be many things. Above all it must be welcoming. There must be somewhere to put coats, hats, umbrellas, wellingtons, gloves and so on. Old houses are not often provided with facilities for hall storage so the organisation of the hall has to be fairly ingenious. A row of hooks and a narrow shelf will be invaluable. If there are stairs you may find room for a telephone or a set of shelves or even a pram or a bicycle under them. The more you can hang up the better because the hall will probably need to be swept more often than any other room in the house and the less you have to move to sweep the better. Try to find room for a mirror so that visitors can have a quick look at themselves before coming in and you can check yourself before going out.

Small spaces require careful thought in detailed planning. The arrangement of this workroom has all the ingenuity of boat planning. The clever angling of the desk enables one to sit without facing dead against the wall. The narrow radiator takes up little space and the chair can be folded against a wall.

Making the most of your space

When you first get your house or flat, don't jump to the conclusion that the most obvious use for a room is necessarily the best one. It may be that in a house that is identical with others in a street, a combination of aspect, prospect, your family needs and other practical considerations may suggest that you plan your accommodation somewhat in reverse.

This has been successfully achieved in the small London terrace house illustrated here. You will see that the placing of the living room on the second floor, where the architect has designed a splendid rooflight, has given the main room in the house a special character which could not have been achieved by having it lower down in the house.

On the opposite side of the street there are taller buildings that would block the afternoon sun from a living room on the ground or first floor – especially in the autumn – whereas one on the second floor would enjoy direct sunlight for longer. From this followed the placing of the dining room and kitchen on the floor below, since it is more satisfactory to have them close to each other. The bedrooms are on the ground floor and basement.

The arrangement is successful from other points of view because when guests come they can leave their coats in the bedroom and wash in the bathroom, both situated conveniently near the front door.

On the other hand, do not – without very good reason – wilfully change a set pattern of use in a house, especially if you plan to live in it in the style of the former occupants. It is a pity not to continue the use for which rooms were originally designed, particularly in houses built before 1840, where the main rooms had delightful mouldings on ceilings and walls, as well as elegant windows.

A common necessity nowadays, however, is to have the kitchen close to the dining room, where formerly it may have been in a basement or banished to some back region. For 'elegant' dining you may not want to be able to see the kitchen, in which case you may choose to build on a conservatory-like addition. This could house the kitchen and provide a breakfast area, as well as being a home for plants. With up-to-date double glazing and sensible heating, such a room need not be cold.

Kitchen replanning is the most common home conversion, and has become such a big industry that you can usually get a manufacturer to plan the layout for you if you give him the measurements of the room. This planning service is often free of charge if you subsequently buy their units. The best buys in kitchen units are self-assembly ones, which you can see advertised in home interest magazines.

Another popular major change is to knock the front and rear ground-floor rooms into one. However, before you do this think about the needs of your household, especially if you have young children who may not like being banished to an icy bedroom to do their homework, and who might in any case enjoy working in a downstairs room while you listen to your hi-fi separately.

Between-the-wars semis of the smaller type quite often have a lavatory on the ground floor and a bathroom on the first floor. You may well want to renew and update all the sanitary fittings and you may even find that one bathroom is not enough. You may not want to lose any of the three bedrooms usually found in this type of house, and may wonder how to install another bathroom within the existing four walls without making further additions. You can, of course, follow the suggestion made on page 26 of taking a slice off each of the two large bedrooms and installing an internal bathroom.

If you are willing to sacrifice the third bedroom (which often measures only 2m by 2.5m anyway), consider using it as a bathroom cum dressing room, perhaps leading off the main bedroom. With this arrangement you can leave the walls and proportions of your main bedroom undisturbed, making it easier to plan not only for sleeping, but as a work/study/private living room as well. Alternatively, if the bedrooms are very small, as you often find in terrace houses of a somewhat earlier date, you might be able to fit clothes cupboards for both rooms over the staircase, sloping the underside to provide the necessary headroom.

The specially designed rooflight floods this top-floor living room with daylight. One small window was retained to provide a view out and avoid a closed-in feeling.

BOOK OF HOME IMPROVEMENTS, READER'S DIGEST LONDON

Modernising a Victorian terrace house

The typical house pattern of two rooms on each floor with a ground-floor rear extension and half-landing bathroom is in use all over the country, but if you are moving into a house and planning alterations, consider a rationalisation of room relationships. For example, do you really want bathrooms at half-landing level, away from the bedrooms, when the ideal pattern is to have bedroom and bathroom adjoining?

A popular conversion to suit a family with two children is shown here. The living room is on the first floor – a pattern established several centuries ago, even in houses not planned with the best room at the front on the first floor. This is often advantageous because of the better light and view.

Building regulations stipulate that all 'habitable' rooms (bedrooms and living rooms) must have a minimum ceiling height of 2.3m. By classifying the two lower rooms in the extension of this house as a utility room and a bathroom (ie not 'habitable') the architect was able to give them ceiling heights of only 2.1m. He then built a third room on top; being under a sloping roof, its height is governed by regulations that allow an even lower ceiling than in non-habitable rooms.

So the former ground-floor kitchen has become a utility room, convenient for the children to play near their mother, but not under her feet. The new kitchen is now next to the dining room. The visitors'/children's bathroom is above the utility room, on the level of the first half landing. On top is the children's bedroom; it is designed as an attic room and is quite adequate for children, who are not very tall, after all.

These photographs and the plans on pages 22 and 23 are of a typical terrace house of medium size, without a basement. A new rear addition on three floors, each opening from the half landing, was specially designed so that the use of the lower rooms (as utility room and bathroom) enabled the ceiling heights to be lower than is usually permitted. In this way the overall height of the extension was kept down to allow daylight to get to the small rear courtyard.

JERRY TUBBY

The existing rooms in the main house were re-organised to enable the kitchen to be next to the dining room, and opening from it. The first-floor front room, which is invariably larger than the ground-floor rooms, is now used (as was originally intended) as the living room.

On the second floor an internal bathroom was inserted between the two bedrooms, thus enabling the master bedroom to have its own bathroom en suite. The guest bedroom shares a bathroom with the new attic bedroom built in the rear extension. The third-floor bedroom in the roof of the main house, newly enlarged by the addition of a twin dormer window, has its own shower and WC fitted into an 84cm by 214cm space between the two chimney stacks.

Thus arranged, the house works conveniently for modern family life, enabling a greater sense of privacy to be achieved than in a house planned on only two floors. Architect: Nicholas Hills

Left: This rear extension houses a ground-floor utility room, a guest/children's bathroom, and an attic bedroom. The simple traditional features blend well with the existing terrace.

1 The second-floor attic bedroom in the rear extension shown opposite. The dormer window gives sufficient headroom but does not eliminate the attractive tent shape.
2 The internal bathroom which leads off the second-floor master bedroom, as shown

on the plan on page 23. Although the room is very small, the mirrors covering the two side walls make it appear many times its actual size.
3 The guest/children's bathroom on the first floor of the rear extension. A marble-topped

wash basin unit has been built into the projecting end window.
4 In the kitchen, standard units have been stained moss green to harmonise with the wall tiles. The rear window was replaced with French doors.

*Plans of the Victorian terrace house
described on pages 20 and 21*

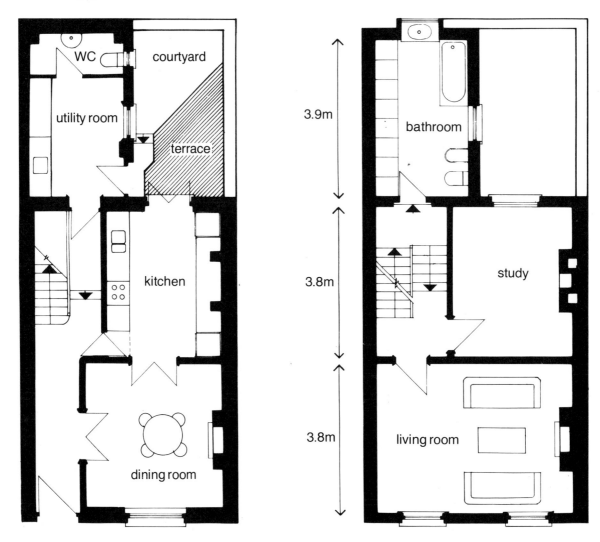

GROUND FLOOR   FIRST FLOOR

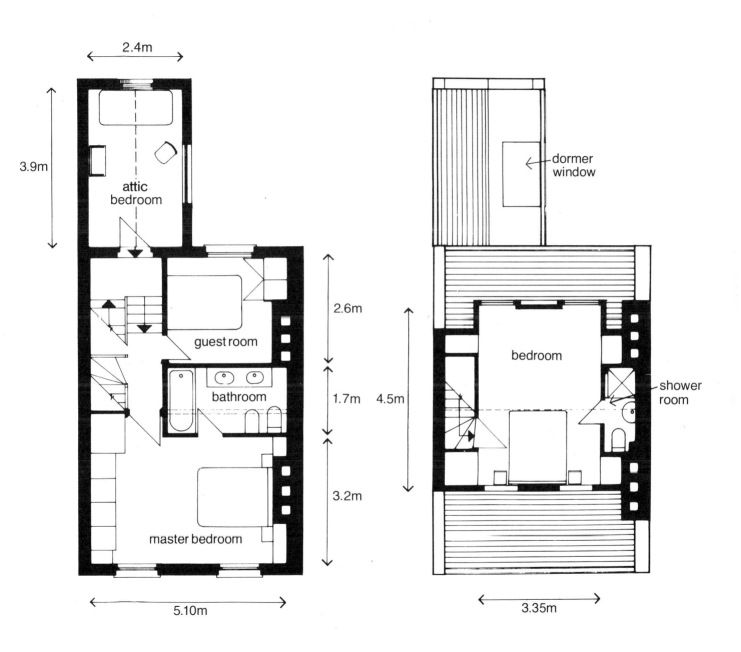

2.4m

3.9m

attic bedroom

guest room

2.6m

bathroom

1.7m

4.5m

master bedroom

3.2m

5.10m

SECOND FLOOR

dormer window

bedroom

shower room

3.35m

THIRD FLOOR

23

Converting a small terrace house into two flats

Even if you have no money saved up for a home, with will and effort you can provide yourself with accommodation that pays for itself. With the help of a friendly bank manager and a bridging loan or mortgage or both, you can buy a small terrace house and convert it into two flats, one of which you let.

In the example shown here, the ground floor was designed as a studio flat with a 'kitchen in a cupboard'. The former kitchen was divided into two; one section was made into a bathroom and the other used to enlarge the main living space. A small rear addition was built, making it possible to fit larger windows across one end.

Remember that you would need to install separate metering for gas and electricity in each flat. Such a conversion could be informal and thus not subject to a rating reassessment, and the rent you charge should cover your mortgage repayments. Later on, if you can afford it, the two flats can be combined into one house again. The extra bathroom will be a welcome addition, and one kitchen can be used as a utility room.

The plans opposite are of a small two-storey terrace house, which has been converted into two flats. The ground floor has been replanned as a studio flat, with the two main rooms knocked into one.

The photographs at right illustrate this studio flat, in which cooking, eating, sleeping and other activities are combined. The sofa converts to a bed, and the bedding is kept in the pine chest nearby. Kitchen units were fitted along the wall flanking the staircase, and are concealed behind sliding and folding louvred doors. There is a separate bathroom at the back.

The first floor has been planned as a one-bedroom flat (not illustrated, but see

plan opposite), with a separate living room at the front. The former bathroom on the half landing was converted into a kitchen/dining room, and a new WC fitted into the space above the stairs. A row of cupboards was built along one wall of the bedroom, incorporating a shower and wash basin. This compact arrangement would be ideal for a young couple.

JERRY TUBBY

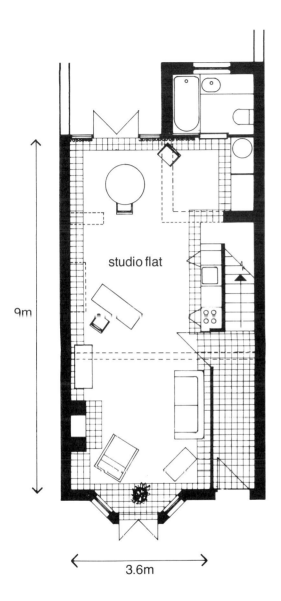

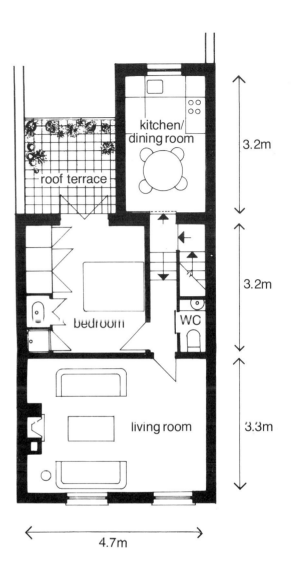

GROUND FLOOR

FIRST FLOOR

**PLAN OF THE FIRST FLOOR OF A LARGE
TERRACE HOUSE BEFORE CONVERSION**

Town flats

In towns you very often find that a single floor of a Georgian or Victorian town house is being used as a flat. If you are able to determine the planning of your flat, these drawings may help you.

Where you have the use of only two rooms, which have to provide space for living room, bedroom, kitchen and bathroom, there are two basic arrangements which you might consider.

First, you could fit a kitchen 'bar' along one wall of the living room, and a 'bathroom in a cupboard' in the bedroom. However, it is not ideal to have a lavatory opening off a bedroom when it is the only one in the flat. One way round this is to have a lavatory at half-landing level.

The second method of planning is to take a slice off each room and form an internal kitchen and bathroom. This only works in larger houses as you do need enough space for two rooms at least 2m square.

The plans on these pages illustrate three approaches to converting the first floor of a typical large terrace house to form a two-bedroom flat (the original layout is shown on the plan at left).

Solution A (see plan at right) involves the minimum of structural alteration. As the kitchen is part of a living space, particular attention has to be paid to design details such as air extraction. A small shower room is shared by the two bedrooms.

In solution B (see plan far right) an internal kitchen and bathroom have been formed by taking a slice off each of the two main rooms. Both these enclosed rooms would need ducted ventilation and good artificial lighting in order to function well.

In both cases the existing staircase has been enclosed by semi-circular walls at landing and half-landing levels, allowing space for small entrance lobbies within each flat.

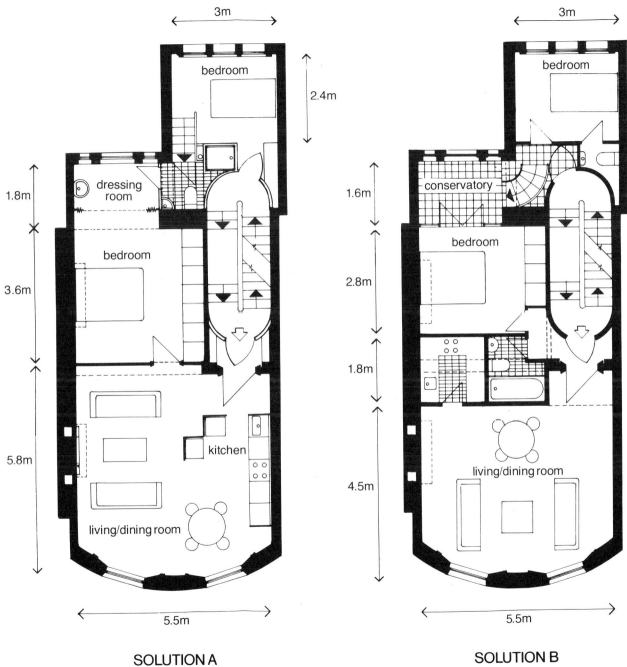

3m

bedroom

2.4m

1.8m

dressing room

3.6m

bedroom

5.8m

kitchen

living/dining room

5.5m

SOLUTION A

3m

bedroom

1.6m

conservatory

2.8m

bedroom

1.8m

4.5m

living/dining room

5.5m

SOLUTION B

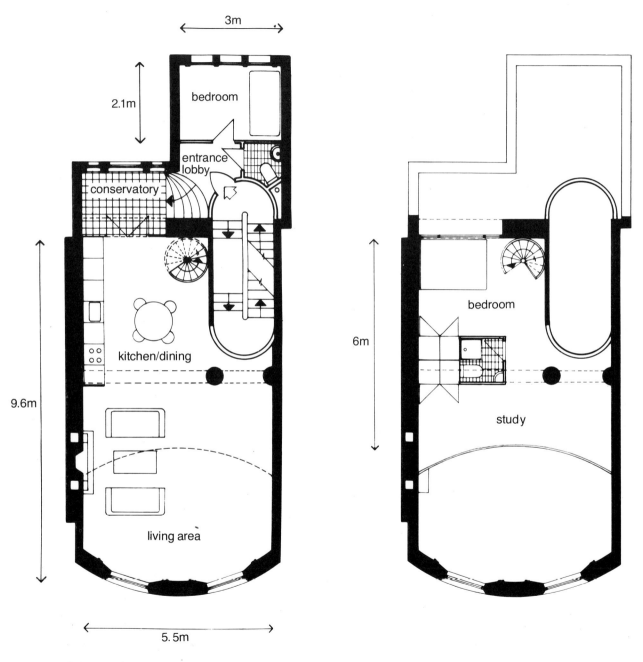

3m

2.1m

bedroom

entrance
lobby

conservatory

9.6m

kitchen/dining

living area

5.5m

SOLUTION C: FIRST FLOOR LEVEL

bedroom

6m

study

BALCONY LEVEL

28

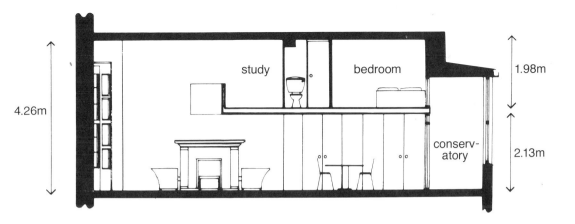

4.26m

study

bedroom

1.98m

conserv-
atory

2.13m

In conversions A and B, shown on pages 26 and 27, a floor-to-ceiling height of about 3·6m has been assumed. If the ceiling is higher – perhaps as much as 4·3m, as is quite often the case on the first floor of large Victorian terrace houses – then an alternative conversion is possible, taking full advantage of the vertical section. You could insert a small gallery or balcony which would provide an upper level for sleeping or studying.

Solution C (see plans opposite and section above) shows how a half floor or balcony can be inserted in a taller room, thus allowing a bedroom, bathroom and study area to sit above the living and dining rooms, reached by a spiral staircase. Such a balcony can be light and demountable – perhaps constructed of scaffolding tubes and planks, as in the photograph at right – or it can be a more permanent structure of steel and timber joists. In either case it would be wise to have the advice of an engineer or architect in designing the support structure.

Pockets of space

Quite often, even in new houses, there are pockets of space – perhaps on a landing, or where a sloping roof adjoins a room, or even a loft or cellar – where you can fit in a variety of functions, leaving other areas free for more varied purposes. Boilers can be moved out of kitchens – where they often seem to be placed for the convenience of the builder rather than the occupier – and fitted into a cupboard in a hall or on a top landing.

Remember that organising any domestic interior requires just as much detailed thought as planning on a larger scale, and the old adage 'a place for everything and everything in its place' has a lot of relevance when you are planning your home.

When you consider how much can be fitted into a well equipped boat or caravan, you can begin to realise that even with limited space it's possible to perform near miracles. It's simply a question of thinking small enough to visualise how each function can fit in.

Landings

Take, for example, a typical left-over space, say at the top of the stairs. You could fit a shower room, as suggested above, or you might turn it into a library corner, and provide a good spotlight for reading and a comfortable stool or folding chair. Alternatively, you could fit a well equipped cleaning centre for boots and shoes.

Other uses for such a space could be as a hobbies corner with bench and shelves; a map or chart area or a print or poster corner, with hinged panels

These photographs show three uses for pockets of space which are often wasted. Above left: This boiler has been concealed inside a cupboard on a landing. This leaves a shelf above for storage of vases (or bottles or filing boxes) and when the cupboard doors are closed (left), the wall has a smooth, neat finish.
Above: This small corner under the stairs

has been arranged to house a telephone, lamp and tiny filing cabinet, as well as a mirror and a chair. There is even cupboard space for telephone books and other equipment.
Above right: This compact bathroom has been fitted very neatly at the top of the stairs. If the space available is very restricted, a small sit-up bath can be installed instead of a full-length model.

such as you find in shop displays and art galleries; a telephone corner; or even a place to do homework. Always make sure there's a good light, because no one will bother to use an ill lit corner.

Basements and attics

Seemingly unusable basements and attics can also be put to good use. One tends to forget that cellars or attics with a low ceiling are ideal playrooms for children, who often enjoy the intimacy of a low-ceilinged room that adults cannot comfortably use. In one such cellar one enterprising boy constructed a marionette theatre which gave him endless hours of amusement. He planned shows, painted scenery, arranged lighting and wrote plays as well as making the puppets themselves.

Rooms in the roof quite often have vertical walls of only 1.25m or 1.5m at the sides, whereas it could well be a vast advantage to incorporate *all* the available triangle of space down to the eaves. Not only is this useful for storage that you can get at easily, but beds can be pushed under the angle of the roof, to be pulled out at night for sleeping. During the day you can gain at least 1.7m² of space (the area of a bed) for more general activities.

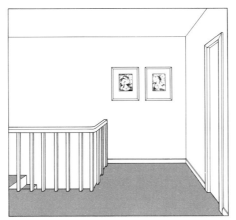

Unused landing space

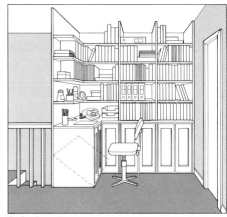

Solution A

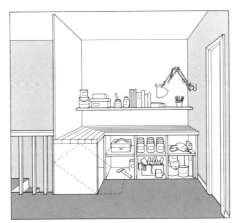

Solution B

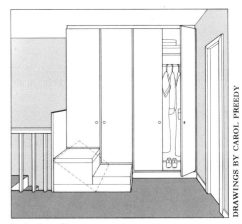

Solution C

DRAWINGS BY CAROL PREEDY

These drawings illustrate three ways in which you might make use of a landing space (shown top left). Each solution utilises the 'dead' space over the top of a flight of stairs rising from the floor below by building out over the staircase, leaving sufficient headroom above the stairs below. In this way a considerable amount of extra space can be put to use, producing in effect an area of wall surface equal to that in a small room. The detailed layout can be arranged in various ways.

Solution A (top right) shows a library corner, which might well be a place where

you can work, with a pull-out desk top and a telephone. Make sure the area is adequately lit and heated, as no one will want to work there if it is cold and dark.

Solution B (above left) shows a hobbies corner, fitted out with a work bench. This might also be where you polish shoes, or store household cleaning equipment.

Solution C (above right) shows a dressing room corner, complete with fitted cupboards. In a small house where there are only two rooms on each floor, and one of those has been converted into a bathroom, a dressing corner could prove invaluable.

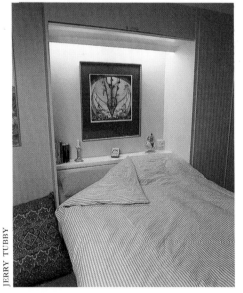

Above left: This London flat is based on the concept of open plan, with tiny bedrooms leading off the main living space; the kitchen is fitted into an angle at right. Diagonal stripes on carpet, blinds and tablecloths provide a geometric contrast to the simple modern architectural design. The circular main bedroom (above) has tented hangings of French mattress ticking cut diagonally; this helps with insulation as well as giving the impression of sleeping in an Arab tent.

Left: A folding bed can be a tremendous space saver in any home, and is particularly suitable in an open-planned space, where an obvious 'bedroomy' look is not wanted. This double bed has a useful shelf for night-time needs when opened out, but is totally camouflaged when folded away into the wall.

Open plan

The concept of open planning – that is, no clear definition of functions within separate rooms – is in a sense inseparable from modern architecture. In one way, although it provided a break from the typical bourgeois house plan, it showed a return to the medieval approach where a whole variety of activities took place in one central hall.

The convenience of this may be in doubt today, when for many people home life tends to be made up of a mixture of work brought home from the office, school homework, television, hi-fi, entertaining and many other pursuits; but as an idea it has lingered on to influence a general approach in house design and conversion, probably because people do like to have a sense of space. When there are only one or two people living in the space, an orderliness and routine can be worked out, but this breaks down when more people – perhaps older children – are involved. You may think that a large family living room will make you feel closer to your family, but you will almost certainly need the ability to retire to a room of your own.

So it makes a lot of sense to plan each bedroom not simply as a sleeping room but in every respect rather like a bedsitting room. The needs of every family vary of course, but if someone has to work at home you should be able to fit in an elegant desk or work table. If your particular activity is untidy, you can build the whole unit into a cupboard with sliding or folding doors to conceal everything when not in use, making it unnecessary to tidy up at night. If your room is small, a fold-away bed is an excellent idea and gives

no hint that the room is a bedroom.

An example of open planning is given in the flat shown on the opposite page. Although this is not easily copied in most existing houses, it nevertheless illustrates an interesting approach to the interior arrangement of any house or flat and may be adaptable to your own special circumstances. The basis of the planning was to provide a series of bays, each with its own lighting and windows, and accessible from three sides. Each bay can become a room of its own, measuring 2.45m by 3.65m. Alternatively, one bay can be combined with others to produce an open-plan living space. Small attic-like rooms which formed part of the original structure of this roof-top flat have been utilised as bedrooms. Although the rooms are small and almost entirely occupied by beds, they are a cosy contrast to the openness of the general living space and form in effect bolt holes for each member of the family to retire to, thus maximising the use of the main space for family activities.

Another feature of the design is the absence of passages. However, passages are important in any shared home, as they improve privacy and increase sound insulation between rooms. Also, there are times when you don't want to pass through the main living area – when rushing naked to answer the telephone, for example. In the flat shown here, this alternative route is provided by the conservatory/kitchen, which is built into the angle of the open living area, providing a by-pass round it.

Open-plan space does not need to be all on one level, of course. You can obtain an open feeling by letting space flow from one floor to another, often

by way of a mezzanine or intermediate level. In the conversion of a small Georgian house (see the plans and section on pages 34 to 37), where the existing staircase took up a quarter of the floor space on each level, the whole thing was demolished and replaced by a central spiral staircase. This left the two rooms on the upper floors as before, but made room for an internal bathroom as well. The ground floor was left open and the floor was cut back 1.25m from the rear wall. This, together with an addition of 1.25m, made it possible to create a mezzanine dining room, level with the garden terrace at the back. The basement, formerly dingy and enclosed, was also opened up and turned into a kitchen and breakfast room. So the general living space of the house worked together on three floors as one unit.

If you're not sure about open plan, this short check list of its advantages and disadvantages might help you to make up your mind.

Pros
1 Open plan gives a more spacious feeling which is good for mental well-being, especially if you are inclined to feel hemmed in by small spaces.
2 It is a good solution for people who have only a small area but want to fit a lot of different activities into it.
3 It is excellent for people who live together, but whose interests and timing are not likely to clash, and for one person living alone.
4 It is good for households with small children, as the children can be kept in sight whatever their parents are doing, rather than being shut away.
5 It is usually cheaper: there are fewer walls to decorate, furnishings to buy.

6 The space may be more adaptable to changing needs: the workspace can be extended or reduced; the kitchen, dining and living areas can merge with each other. The hi-fi system will reach you wherever you are without extra speakers (you can use headphones when this would not be an advantage).

7 People who are cooking, sewing or doing any other job need not be cut off from the other people and happenings in the house.

Cons

1 It can be unfortunate if everyone's interests and timing do not coincide. It is difficult if one person wants to type while someone else would rather read, and disastrous if there's an actual clash of interests such as a piano and a record player.

2 Don't underestimate the lack of privacy. If there are separate bedrooms (see page 33) it's not a serious problem, but otherwise it is asking a great deal of people living in the open-plan space.

3 Smells: bacon fat permeating from the kitchen area can be intolerable. Nappy and other strong smells must be kept separate, though you can partly overcome a smell problem by installing an extractor fan.

4 Unless you are very well organised and fairly neat your home could become a slum. You need well planned storage and plenty of it and the discipline to keep everything in its place.

5 Noise is one of the major drawbacks, especially with older children in the house, when you no longer have much control over the hours they go to bed and what they do with their free time.

6 You have to heat the whole area, and if it is very large this could work out expensive. It is therefore less economical than a conventional house arrangement where rooms can be heated individually.

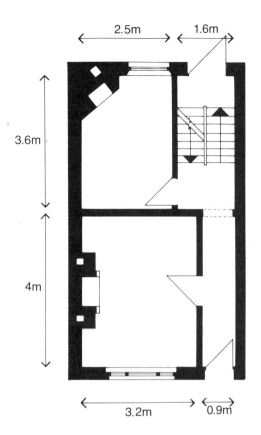

BASIC ORIGINAL FLOOR PLAN

The plans on these pages show how a typical terrace house with a frontage of only 4·25m has been replanned inside to provide a sense of space in the living areas with the convenience of having a bathroom next to each of the bedrooms.

The section (opposite) reveals how the ground-floor and basement rooms have been combined as one flowing space, with a mezzanine created at garden level, where

the floor has been cut back 1·2m and the building extended by 1·2m to provide a terrace room used for dining.

The new spiral staircase takes up far less space than the original conventional staircase, and its central position keeps circulation space to a minimum.

A wine cellar was provided under the dining room, and a newly added attic floor serves as a study.

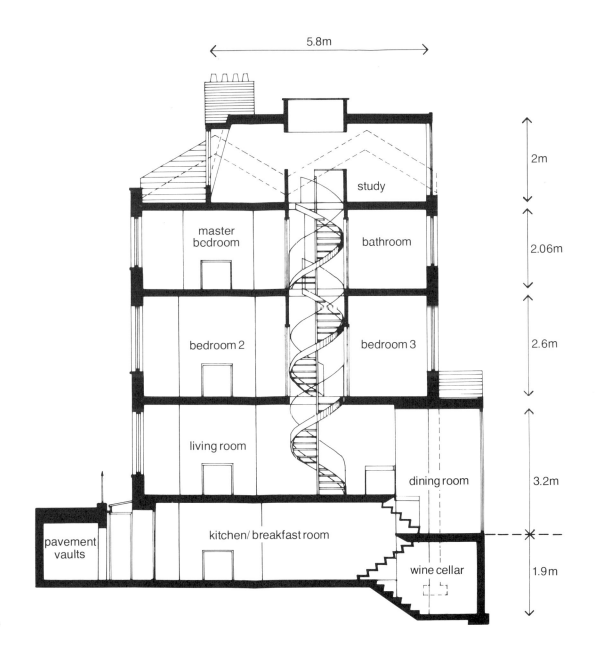

5.8m

2m

2.06m

2.6m

3.2m

1.9m

study

master bedroom

bathroom

bedroom 2

bedroom 3

living room

dining room

pavement vaults

kitchen/ breakfast room

wine cellar

35

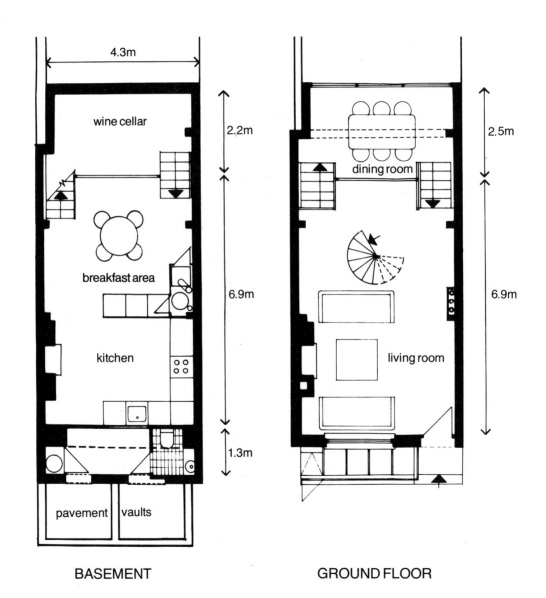

4.3m

wine cellar

2.2m

breakfast area

6.9m

kitchen

1.3m

pavement | vaults

BASEMENT

dining room

2.5m

living room

6.9m

GROUND FLOOR

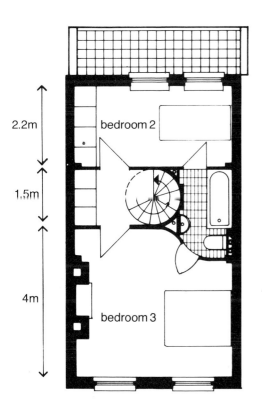

2.2m

1,5m

4m

bedroom 2

bedroom 3

FIRST FLOOR

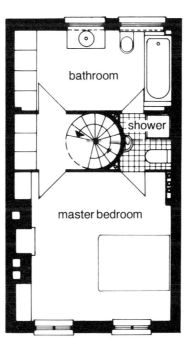

bathroom

shower

master bedroom

SECOND FLOOR

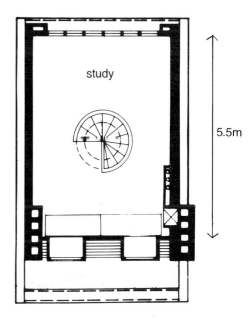

study

5.5m

THIRD FLOOR

Detailed planning

Doors

The detailed elements of your home have an important bearing on the convenience of your life. For example, a door in the wrong place, of the wrong width, which opens the wrong way and is made of the wrong material can cause constant annoyance. If you are planning alterations, consider whether a door should be in the corner of a room, or placed centrally on a wall. If it is in a corner make sure it is spaced out a bit so that you can open it at least a little more than 90° for getting furniture through. Most items of modern furniture knock down and even divan bed bases fold, so consider if you really need, say, a 750mm wide door or whether a 600mm door would be wide enough, leaving extra wall space for furniture and fittings.

The door itself is important too. One of the reasons we have doors is for sound proofing, so when choosing a flush door have one with a solid core. Flush doors are seldom very handsome in themselves and if painted they often look scruffy in no time. For a few extra pounds you can have veneered doors which can take polish. A hessian-faced door can be cross banded with ribbons to make a useful notice board for invitations, postcards and cuttings.

If you are starting from scratch and thinking about handles, try to line them up with adjacent light switches. One metre from the floor is a good height for both. Generally speaking, unless you are restoring a period house, avoid over-fancy or reproduction door handles and hinges and choose simple classic aluminium fittings or the cheaper versions made of brightly coloured plastics.

It is very frustrating to hang a door only to have to remove it later when the carpets are laid. You can avoid this either by fitting rising butt hinges, which

Above: Folding doors which slide neatly out of the way are good dividers for a wide opening. They are particularly convenient in a large family house, where a space can be divided to enable two activities to take place without either disturbing the other. Left: An attractive and practical approach to displaying current correspondence and messages: a door covered in felt and cross banded with ribbon and drawing pins.

carry a door over a carpet, or by leaving a small clearance between the floor and the bottom of the door when it is hung. It is smarter to have doors of only one type in a house, usually hinged or (less often) sliding. Sliding doors need careful detailing to ensure a good sound-proof fit, and conversions from hinged to sliding doors are seldom satisfactory. An alternative to a sliding door is a bi-folding door, which is in two halves, hinged in the middle as well as at one edge, and controlled by a guide in a track at the top. Use this type of door only if you have to, for example in a cramped bathroom or lavatory, where the door cannot open inwards and is inconvenient if opened out. They are also useful for cupboards.

In a kitchen, where you may have a door opening into a garden or courtyard or into a dining room, a stable door is often a practical feature. This is a door that is split horizontally in half, enabling the bottom part to be closed when the upper half is open, like a window. It is useful for keeping children and animals in (or out) or merely under surveillance, while you enjoy fresh air and sunlight.

Internal doors can be glazed to let more light into a dark room, and they are also useful for separating an entrance lobby or leading into a living room where privacy is not essential. You can buy glass doors made from a single sheet of toughened glass, either plain, tinted or obscured, which can be fitted into an ordinary opening. These doors certainly have their uses, but when badly chosen can make your home seem too much like the inside of a seaside boarding house.

One final word on doorways. If you have one you want to block off, you can save yourself money by not having the door taken away and leave yourself the option of utilising it in the future, by 'jibbing' it on the room side. That is, making it flush, taking off the

architraves and treating it as wall. On the hall side you can fit a full-length sheet of mirror over the door. This makes a good feature, and helps to brighten and seemingly widen the hall.

You may not often have to concern yourself about external doors, but whatever you do, don't change from the prevailing pattern in the street. If your front door is in bad condition, get it repaired or copied and paint or polish it to a good colour. In spite of the current fashion for gaily painted front doors, the traditional colour of very dark green or a greeny-grey or white is classically smart. Old pine doors can be stripped by sending them away to be 'pickled' and this can be done in one day so you need not be without a door for long. Clean off all chemicals carefully then seal and polish or repaint it. Old, even much patched pine doors look full of character if they are simply varnished with clear marine varnish and the iron knobs and knockers replaced or painted black. Although it may look fresh for a while, new brasswork will eventually need either constant cleaning or repolishing and lacquering.

If your house has an integral garage or one built at the side of the house, garage doors are something you can often replace to advantage. There has been a considerable advance in door mechanisms over the past 30 years and, rather than put up with the tedium of side-hung double doors, you might fix an up-and-over door. The door itself can be in almost any pattern you like, but again consider the style of the house and the effect of the door design on it.

At the same time as replacing the door you should consider an additional use to which your garage might be put. You could glaze the door and use the garage as a children's playroom or party room when the car is out. A tarpaulin or polythene sheet can be rolled out to catch any oil when the car returns. A garage used in this way would be more practical if you insulated the ceiling (if separate from the house) and you could lay ceramic tiles on the floor, or cork or vinyl if the floor is dry.

Windows

As with doors, there is a great deal of technical detail that goes to make a successful window. Unless you are building a house and have a chance to discuss the details with your architect, think carefully before altering the design or size of a window. This is not so important at the back of a house, but remember that a window is part of a house with a specific architectural style; if the formerly uniform windows of every house in the street were cut and changed about, the impression from outside could seem like visual anarchy.

Fortunately the most frequent changes are the insertion of French doors or double glazed patio doors at the back of the house, where this is for the most part acceptable. If you are simply making a French door where formerly there was a simple window, you need only cut away the brickwork under the sill, take out the old frame and put in a new one with (preferably) double-glazed sealed units. Take care to see there is a proper damp-proof membrane of either bituminous felt or metal under the sill, which should itself be of a hardwood such as iroko. There should also be a water bar slotted into the bottom of the sill to prevent any capillary action from conducting water inside the house. In these days of frequent house burglary, make sure from the start that you have good locks on both windows and doors.

Fireplaces

The concept of the family hearth is part of man's instinct and this is why the history of the fireplace and its changing fashions exactly parallels the history of fashion in clothes. An architectural historian can date to within a few years a particular moulding on, say, a gothic chimney jamb in the same way that a fashion expert can date a garment.

In countries where a fireplace is not needed as a functional element (and curiously the history of western civilisation has been carried on for the most part in countries where it *is*), concentration is centred on that other means of providing heat and light to an interior, the window. Today, because of central heating, the fireplace is an optional feature in the living room, but we still feel the need to provide a focus for family life. For many people this is provided by television, but a television set should not be thought of as an important visual focus when designing a room, but an intrusion of the outside world into the home.

Our towns and cities are much cleaner and healthier places to live in since the demise of the open fire. Now it is usual to find only a flue from a gas central heating boiler in a newly built house, whereas formerly at least four chimneys (one serving each main room) would have existed. In spite of this, the popularity of the open fire in one form or another does not wane.

So if you are fortunate enough to live in an older house with open fireplaces, think carefully before taking them out, and remember that before removing a flue you need a special certificate from the local district surveyor or building inspector, as flues often provide essential buttressing to a party or external wall. It is likely that you will want to keep at least one open fire, probably in the living room, but it is also delightful to have a fire in the dining room, if only at Christmas. Certainly if your house is old, and the chimney piece is attractive, do not touch it. Who knows, but in a few years we shall need open fires again to keep us warm?

Don't forget either that fireplaces can be fitted with back boilers or the more efficient types of wood burning stove (except in smokeless zones), so it is important to keep the flues intact. In some old terrace houses the flues interconnect with those of the neighbouring house so you may not be allowed to remove any of the brickwork at all.

However, if you have decided to remove a fireplace, perhaps in a small bedroom or bathroom, and gain nearly half a square metre extra, you can often remove just the central part of the chimney breast; leaving the two side piers of brickwork. This opening can be extended upwards to door head height and a valuable space for a cupboard or a fitted wash basin unit provided. If the room is a bathroom or kitchen, you can make use of the old flue by fitting an extractor fan into it, but take care to sweep all the chimneys first. Alternatively you can use the space as a niche to display a special piece of sculpture or furniture, fit bookshelves or even build in a larder, making good use of the ventilation from the old flue.

Below: The clean-cut lines of this circular fireplace with stainless steel frame suit the simple, modern design of the house.
Designer: Max Glendinning
Right: This traditional fireplace with decorated surround and tiled hearth is ideal for a small Victorian terrace house.

TIM STREET-PORTER/ELIZABETH WHITING

ROB MATHESON

Shelves

Most people like to have some storage for books in their living room, as few of us have enough to merit using a room solely as a library. For some people, books are as important a means of indicating their character and interests as the colour of a shirt. But you should never fall into the trap of buying books for show. Too many book clubs offer flashily bound books of 'the classics' which one suspects are seldom read. On the other hand, shelf after shelf of paperbacks are not *that* attractive to look at and so shouldn't dominate a focal point in the room. Remember that books look better with their spines lined up with the front of the shelf.

The most usual place to fit bookshelves is on either side of a chimney breast. The side walls provide ready fixings for the simplest bookshelves – especially helpful for the do-it-yourself enthusiast – and the books have an orderly appearance, as they are contained between the rigid verticals of the side walls. However, if there is no chimney breast, the best place may be flanking the window. This arrangement can be very successful, as it helps to frame the window and at the same time uses space that is often wasted. The idea can be developed to provide a rather dull window with a window seat, and you may be able to improve the proportion of width to height at the same time.

Bookshelves at low level are often not such a good idea; not only do they take up space that could be used for furniture, but you also have to keep bending down to get at the books. Especially in recently built houses, where the ceiling height conforms closely to the prescribed minimum, a large object such as a bookcase set across the wall only emphasises the room's lack of height by 'layering' it horizontally, and spoils the overall appearance.

Without doubt the simplest type of shelving is the one in which slotted metal uprights are screwed to the wall with adjustable brackets slotted in them to support the shelves. Remember to choose thick enough shelves so that they do not sag under the weight of the books; as a rough guide 25mm blockboard needs to be supported about every 600mm. If your shelves are to be 1m long, you should provide some support 150mm from each end.

Bookshelves are about the simplest item of furniture you can make, the most basic form being chipboard planks supported on bricks. If you are planning something more elaborate, they usually look better if they run in vertical sections of 600mm to 1m wide. If your house is old, and has 200mm skirting boards and a cornice, you can add an elegant detail by supporting the bottom shelf on the top of the skirting,

Left: Close-up view of metal upright-and-bracket shelving supports, a flexible and unobtrusive system made by Tebrax which is suitable for any room in the house. Below: The worktop of this home-made desk comprises two sheets of thick glass with a map sandwiched between. The suede-covered pedestals supporting it are fitted with bookshelves for handy reference. An angled lamp provides good light.

and sloping back the sides and bottom fascia at 45 degrees. You can do the same at the top, sloping the sides back to the cornice. In this way you do not interrupt the visual flow of the mouldings round the room and your bookcase looks built in rather than an ad-hoc addition (see drawing 2 on the opposite page).

Opposite: Two ingenious methods of dealing with the wall area round a plain window. Above: A feature has been made of an offset window, typical of a back room in a Victorian house, by fitting bookcases at each side with a window seat between. A louvred shutter covers the blank wall area. Below: A high window is transformed with fitted bookshelves and a window seat.

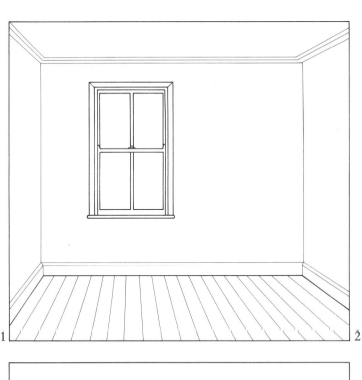

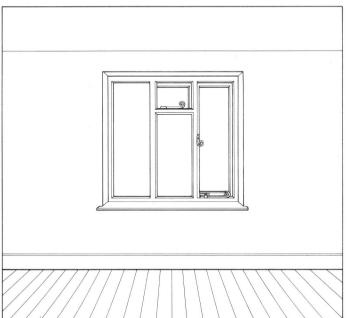

DRAWINGS BY CAROL PREEDY

43

Major alterations

One of the most common types of house, apart from modern estate houses, is the between-the-wars 'semi'. These exist all around almost every town and city in Great Britain, just one ring further out than their Victorian or Edwardian counterparts. They can be very pleasant to live in, with a well established environment, stable neighbourhood, good communications and developed 'arcadian' planting (many streets of this period were planted with trees).

Unfortunately, in some areas the external character of many of these houses is being spoiled. One mistake their owners sometimes make is to replace the original windows, which often used to have stained glass in the fanlights, with 'picture windows' that picture nothing more than an urban road and that are invariably draped with nylon net curtains.

If you buy an elderly house, treat it as you would any other antique: with a certain amount of respect, for its external character at least. Any alterations to the front of a house that is uniform with others in a row should be considered very carefully. These include painting brickwork, altering front doors, adding inappropriate

Above right: One house in this simple terrace has been modernised, with disastrous consequences. The bow window is quite out of keeping, and the changed shape of the upper windows alters the proportions – not for the better.
Right: The houses in this Victorian terrace have not been tampered with, but have been left as originally designed. Regular painting keeps them looking smart.
Far right: The old ceramic tiles on the walls and floor of this porch have been left in their original splendour.

JOHN PRIZEMAN

JERRY TUBBY

KARIN CRADDOCK

porches, altering the window design, and adding false shutters, bits of wrought iron, reproduction carriage lamps and plastic awnings. Your money would be better spent on more suitable finishes inside the house.

The two most common methods of extending a house are to build an addition at the back and to add rooms at the top, the most frequent being the ground-floor rear extension. Under the General Development Order of 1973 any house as originally built can have ten per cent of its cubic content added to it. (But if your house was built recently, there may be a condition attached to the planning consent that no further additions may be made.)

Almost without exception, the firms who deal in 'ready-made' extensions produce designs of extraordinary banality. Many people attempt their own, armed with a book like the *Reader's Digest Book of Home Improvements*, which can be very helpful. But for a properly thought-out addition that enhances not only the visual aspect of your house but also its value, it would be better to ask an architect to produce a design for you, even if you intend to do the actual building yourself.

There are two main approaches to adding to a house. One, which ultimately affects the resale value as well, is to design the addition to be in the same style as and compatible in character with the existing house. Think of it as an alteration to a garment – it would look incongruous to have one green sleeve on a red coat.

When houses were altered in the past, the designer would make the addition 'belong' to the existing fabric so that it was often hard to see exactly which part was built originally and which added. The photograph at right shows an addition to a Hampstead house built so much in the spirit of the original that it appears to have been there always. It is

subtle in other ways too, in that the front of the existing house already provided a balanced composition, so the new façade at the side was played down by bringing the eaves line down to first-floor level and creating a sloping mansard roof.

At the back of the house there was an L-shaped projection on one side which was copied so as to create a symmetrical plan. Such conformist architecture is good manners outside but does not mean that the interior need be dull. The ceiling of the bedroom under the roof of the new projecting wing follows the line of the pitch with all the

These photographs of the inside and outside of a house extension show how unobtrusive this treatment can be. The beamed bedroom ceiling echoes the shape of the roof.

JERRY TUBBY

structural timbers revealed to create a pavilion-like room of great charm, while the adjoining bathroom is contained under the sloping roof at the front of the house.

An alternative approach is to contrast your new extension with the style of the existing house. Such an approach needs a designer with flair, taste and grit. Flair because the new extension should complement the existing house, not be an addition which makes it look either silly or uncomfortable or dwarfed in scale; taste because the materials of which the extension is built should contrast pleasingly with the house, not vie for attention; and grit because, especially in conservation areas in towns and cities, he may have to fight much harder to get his design accepted by the planning authority.

At the other end of the scale, and especially as your first home may well be in the inner city, you may want to demolish an extension at the back that is unsightly or unstable or both. This may provide extra light and garden space; generally speaking there is no problem in doing it. The various rooms demolished (often the kitchen and bathroom) are then relocated within the limits of the existing house.

One point to watch, however, is that listed building consent to demolish should be applied for if your house is within a conservation area. Since rear additions are usually just that, and not part of the original design, you will probably not meet with a refusal. It is unlikely that you will want to demolish other parts of the house, but sometimes a detail like an oriel window may be unstable or unwanted, and consent to remove this will be required as well as planning permission to replace it with a window of a different design.

JERRY TUBBY

The tongued-and-grooved wall cladding follows the pitch of the roof to make the most of the interesting shape of this attic bathroom. The outside view of this extension, which houses a garage with a bedroom and bathroom above, is shown on page 45. Architect: Nicholas Hills

Decorating and furnishing

Once you have planned the basic layout of your home and have completed any structural alterations, the next thing to do is to line your shell: decorate the rooms, dress the windows, cover the floors and plan the lighting.

It is difficult to lay down firm rules for such basics as the use of colour and internal finishes. Unless you have a trained or natural eye for colour, or can repeat a formula that is familiar to you, you will be nervous about making blunders. It is sad that, with the excellent start we give our children at primary school, we let them down so badly later on in terms of understanding design and architecture.

Textured surfaces are very important inside a house, not just for their look and feel and contrast with other textures, but also for sound absorbency and the effect they have on colour. Smooth, shiny surfaces look and feel colder than soft shaggy ones, for example, and most rooms will need a balance. Modern tubular steel furniture with its smooth,

shiny surfaces and sharp, clearly defined lines will contrast well with shaggy-pile carpet and rough-textured fabrics. Experiment with textures when looking for fabrics; if you are choosing for effect rather than practicality, it shouldn't be too difficult. By providing enough soft surfaces to absorb a certain amount of sound you can help make a living room welcoming rather than stiffly formal.

Any architect will tell you that an all-white or off-white room provides an ideal background for a variety of colours and textures, but it might be a mistake to paint a room facing north dead white, or any other cold colour like ice blue or pale green. Remember that a small square of colour on a paint card will be vastly more powerful when put on the four walls of a room, as each

A successful way of breaking up a large area of plain wall is shown in this hall, where a dado rail has been fixed to the wall and textured Lincrusta hung below it.

47

wall tends to reflect its neighbour and the intensity of colour increases.

As a general rule, small rooms need small patterns. There are several firms producing these and many are fresh and charming. Larger rooms can take more powerful colours, but too much of a strong colour can produce a sort of 'colour sickness' which has an unpleasant effect. If there is a large area of plain wall, and especially in a room that is taller than it is wide, you can use a border to improve its proportions.

Another way of breaking up a large wall surface is by fitting a dado rail. This is most effective in rooms over 2.75m high, as any room with a lower ceiling height will probably not need the walls divided horizontally in this way. A dado rail, which is simply a piece of moulded wood similar to a door architrave, is usually positioned about 860mm from the floor. Any strong texture or colour is then confined to one part of the wall – usually the lower part – and the other painted a paler colour, or a neutral such as beige. This produces a rather traditional effect, as shown in the photograph on page 47, which is perfect if you have Victorian or antique furniture. Apart from improving the room's proportions in this way, a dado rail also serves to prevent chair backs from rubbing against the wall.

Paint is probably the cheapest wall-covering. Most shops have a mixing system so you can actually get almost any shade of colour you want. Most paints are washable, and emulsion or similar matt or semi-gloss paints are usually the most satisfactory for internal decoration. If you have bare brick walls you might like to leave them unpainted, in which case you might be wise to seal them so that they don't collect dust. Rather than paint your walls a flat colour, it is possible to 'drag' paint them or 'rag-roll' the paint finish on. This is especially successful in older houses as it has character, and

does not look quite so dead as flat paint. The technique is to apply a coat of matt white oil paint, and then roll on a coat of coloured glaze. This is made from a mixture of oils, driers and colour, in a jelly-like base which prevents it from running. After applying it you either take a stiff brush and run vertical drag lines down the wall, or use a roller covered in dry rags cut into strips, then roll the surface to provide any degree of stippled effect you desire. If you do not feel you can attempt this, a similar effect can be achieved by hanging a jaspé paper.

Other wallcoverings, such as hessian, felt and various textiles – paper backed for ease of hanging, but cheaper if not – are excellent for covering old walls that are irregular or uneven. However,

Matchboarding on the walls combines with the wooden louvred cupboard doors and stripped pine chest of drawers to give this bedroom a warm, comfortable appearance.

JERRY TUBBY

don't expect such coverings to hide large cracks, or to hold together loose plaster. If you have, say, old lath and plaster walls which are nearly collapsing, hack out the plaster, fix new plaster lath board (about 300mm wide) and have a plasterer resurface it for you. Plaster is not expensive and the crispness of the finish is worth the effort.

In rooms that are designed for a specific purpose, choosing a wall-covering is a more complicated problem, for example in a kitchen, where you will probably want washable surfaces. However, even if you choose a laminated or other hard and tough finish for your work surfaces and tile the wall behind the cooker in ceramics or use a gloss or other washable paint, you can still use softer materials on other surfaces to provide a balance. Curtains will naturally help here, but you could also achieve the required effect by using a textured wallcovering on other walls, or cork on the floor or on some walls. Heavy textures, however, will retain cooking smells, and felt or hessian can retain the smell of cigarette smoke for ever. Always ventilate a room by leaving the door or window open at the end of the evening. Acoustically it is better to have some absorbent surfaces or sound gets bounced backwards and forwards.

Matchboarding (tongued and grooved pine, for instance) can be used for walls. This is an expensive wallcovering, but it does insulate very well and gives a room a very warm 'enclosed' feeling. Another possibility is wood panelling.

Ceramic tiles make an excellent wall for bathrooms or for the wall behind a cooker. The coloured and patterned ones are fairly expensive, but plain 100mm² tiles are still cheap and you can fix them yourself quite easily. Try making your own designs using different coloured or patterned tiles.

A ceiling can either match the walls or it can be painted in a contrasting colour. A ceiling with mouldings will

Above left: A small and simple kitchen with smooth, non-absorbent wall, floor and ceiling finishes which are both easy to clean and easy to look at.
Left: A spectacular way of making the most of ceramic tiles: by outlining each wall area with complementary border tiles. The floor finish is carried on over the bath panel.
Above: A splendid patchwork of Victorian wall tiles. This is a good way of using up old tiles, though it would take time and money to collect enough.

49

often look well if it is painted in one colour with the mouldings picked out in white. If the ceiling is very low, stick to pale colours. If it's high (but only if it's very high or if it's a large room split up) you could make a false ceiling. This will help to keep down fuel bills, make the room cosier generally, but shouldn't, of course, be done with a room whose proportions are perfect. Another advantage of bringing a ceiling down is that you can put recessed lighting into it. This is sensible if the old ceiling is in bad condition or if the mouldings are broken. If there's a gap of over 760mm between the new and old ceilings, consider leaving trap doors for storage. Another reason for fitting a false ceiling could be to provide sound insulation between two flats. But if your sole intention is to improve the room's proportions, consider raising the floor rather than lowering the ceiling.

It is always better to paint woodwork white; this is traditional. It acts like white collar and cuffs on a shirt, in defining the architectural details in a room. (It is equally traditional and invariably right to paint all metalwork black, at least outside the house. This applies particularly to railings and balustrades.)

As with any mouldings round a door or window (architraves or frames), all ceiling cornice mouldings, skirtings and dado rails should run *continuously* round a room without interruption. Where a part of a cornice is missing, or if a room has been divided into two, always make the effort to replace the missing length.

You may find that the skirtings, architraves and other joinery are badly dented and damaged. It is often cheaper (and certainly quicker) to take them off altogether and renew them, rather than try to strip badly marked woodwork, which may have several layers of ancient paint on it. You can buy lengths of timber for skirtings from builders' merchants or timber

yards; it's best to get those with already mitred ends. Alternatively you can use skirtings made of chipboard or plywood faced with plastics laminate, which are easier to maintain.

From the welter of ideas for decorating your home that assail you from all directions, we have tried to distil an essence that will give you a formula to work to. You may like patterned wallpaper (and some are useful, especially for period interiors), but in order to create a simple modern interior we have found that by confining pattern to one plane only – the floor – the effect can be exciting without being overpowering and 'busy'. Pattern used on more than one plane can create a visual 'muddle' especially when you have paintings and hangings on the walls; these always look more effective when hung against a plain surface, as any museum curator will tell you.

A sense of spacial continuity is best achieved by continuing one colour throughout a house. So begin by painting your walls white or a pale beigy cream, the ceiling either white or the same colour as the walls, and have as exciting a carpet as you like. This leaves you with only the curtains and soft furnishings to choose; these should be complementary to each other and to the basic scheme.

Dressing windows

Curtains are expensive to have made but not difficult to make yourself; your local library is almost certain to have a book explaining how.

Picture windows usually benefit from wall-to-wall curtaining. This takes a lot of fabric and can be very expensive, but you can always use an old bedspread or sheet or second-hand jumble curtains for a time.

More traditional windows with small panes are usually taller than they are wide and lend themselves to heavier, more sophisticated fabrics. In living rooms these look well hanging from big Victorian curtain rails with wooden rings. You can still sometimes find these in junk and antique shops and some are now available in department stores too. In rooms with smaller windows, crisp printed cotton curtains can look very pretty made just big enough to cover the window when drawn.

If the window has a sill you want to use for putting things on, make sure the curtains hang far enough in front so that they won't knock anything off when being drawn across, or use a roller blind instead.

Quite often blinds may be a more suitable way of covering windows. They are cheap, don't take up space and can be fitted inside the window recess. There are some very pretty papery and slatted ones on the market and many plain coloured or patterned ones to order from department stores. Venetian blinds can be satisfactory, either the traditional horizontal ones or the newer, wider ribbed vertical ones which are most suitable for large, modern squarish windows.

Problem windows, that is those that look too small for the room or look onto a miserable area, can be dealt with in various ways. You can put in a set of shelves with plants on them, thus letting in a little light but

not the awful view, or you could put in a panel of stained glass (or make your own); frosted glass will screen an ugly view but can be rather ugly itself.

These drawings illustrate four bold and practical ways of dressing a small window using blinds. All made by Sunway Blinds and available from good department stores

Flooring

The flooring in your house is one of the most expensive things you will have to buy, so you can't afford to make mistakes. It's useful to know what would be the best flooring for each situation. Probably the cheapest way to tackle wooden floorboards is to sand and seal them. You can hire a sander fairly cheaply from a hire service shop; there are branches throughout the country (look in the Yellow Pages). If there are draughts coming up through gaps in the floorboards, take them up and re-lay them closer together. After sanding, you can finish them with a wood seal. Bright colours are sometimes more fun than traditional 'wood' shades and you can achieve dramatic effects by staining alternate boards to enhance their decorative linear pattern.

The sanding is a bit of a chore: loud, vibrating and dusty, but not difficult. The seal itself is not expensive and it shouldn't take more than a few days to complete the job, even if you apply three or four coats. The finish is not everlasting in a room that takes a lot of traffic; in a hall or kitchen, say, you may have to re-sand the floor every three years or so. But it should last much longer in a living room or bedroom, especially if you use rugs as well. Eventually, if you decide you want and can afford some more sophisticated form of floorcovering, you will not have wasted money on something cheap and shoddy in the meantime.

Here is a simple list of some of the floorcoverings available. Each type is produced in various qualities; it is not always necessary to get the most expensive. Choice should depend on whether the floor is going to get a lot of rough treatment, whether it will need a lot of cleaning and so on. Bedroom carpet need not be as tough as living room or passage carpet and thinner vinyl tiles may be quite adequate in a little used lavatory though you should get the thickest and best quality for a hall or kitchen. Carpet squares are widely available. They measure about 3m or 4m square, and usually have a border. They are cheaper than fitted carpet (and can show off sanded and sealed boards round the edges).

Carpet helps to retain warmth and diminish sounds from clomping boots and shoes. There are carpets available now in man-made fibres which are satisfactory for kitchens and bathrooms. Carpet tiles may be the best answer for a kitchen. Some firms make loose-laid carpet tiles in different grades; some have rubber backs and can be picked up individually to be washed and dried when they get dirty.

When buying carpet look for the British Standard 3655 label (which you'll find on most British carpets) which will give you an idea of its size, construction, fibre content and cleaning requirements. In many ways wool is still the best for appearance and for keeping clean but you can get perfectly good quality carpets made of man-made fibres or mixtures of man-mades and wool. These are usually cheaper and the price may make up your mind for you.

If you can't see a carpet you like in the shop's ordinary range, ask to see their contract range – domestic designs are beginning to get simpler and more imaginative in colour but contract ranges offer a wider choice. They are usually of the toughest quality so are generally expensive. When buying stair carpet, buy enough to be able to move the whole carpet down from time to time so that it doesn't wear out on the treads.

Whatever carpet you choose it's important that it should have the correct backing. Rubber-backed and

Above: A cheap way of treating wooden floorboards is to sand and seal them, bringing out the warm tones of the wood. Right: Sheet vinyl with a traditional tile design provides a comfortable and waterproof flooring for this bathroom.

certain tufted carpets can be laid directly onto the floor, but most other kinds must have proper underlay. Newspapers or an old carpet are not satisfactory substitutes. Anything woven will cause the carpet to creep.

Before making a final choice, it's worth having a look round local discount carpet stores, but make sure you don't pay in underlay what you have saved on the carpet.

Vinyl and cork are both excellent for bathrooms, kitchens, children's rooms and entrance halls. Available in both tile and sheet form, vinyl is waterproof and easy to keep clean. The choice of designs is enormous, from flowery patterns to mock ceramic tiles and even bricks. Many people find the soft 'cushion' type very comfortable.

Cork is available in many different tones of brown and in varying thicknesses. It must be given some sort of finish; it can be sealed in the same way as a sanded floor, or polished with

wax polish. Alternatively, you can buy cork tiles coated with pvc, which are especially suitable for bathroom and hall floors that are liable to get wet and/or dirty, and which make polishing or sealing unnecessary.

Wood block is a good looking but expensive covering for a floor. There are various types, the cheapest and most popular being the mosaic kind. There are various woods to choose from and in some cases you can lay it yourself onto a cement screed. Some flooring specialists sell do-it-yourself kits for this kind of flooring as well as other types which have to be laid professionally.

Coir, sisal and rush matting are all pretty and cheap floorcoverings. On the whole they are not suitable for kitchens and bathrooms, because they are difficult to clean and dry, nor for halls where mud and dust brought in will get underneath them and also be hard to clean off. But they are very attractive in living rooms and bedrooms.

Ceramic floor tiles are not cheap, but are luxurious looking, tough and easy to clean. Most department stores have a good range to choose from.

Lighting

Light is important to our comfort, both mental and physical. Lighting in the home needs careful thought and planning. It is more or less accepted now that a single light bulb hanging from the middle of the ceiling is not satisfactory, but houses are still being built with just that in most rooms.

If you have biggish windows, use the daylight that comes through them; don't shut out the light with heavy curtains. If you need to keep out the glare of a hot sun, blinds are ideal.

From the safety point of view, all stairs must be lit so that there's no shadow falling on them, from bannisters, say. All steps, corners, passages and low doorways must be lit so that people don't constantly trip or knock themselves. Such lighting needn't be very bright and should be diffused and general so as not to cast heavy shadows. You may find that many such places are adequately lit from a window during the day but that you need some sort of lighting at night.

Other than safety lighting there are basically two sorts of lighting: decor lighting, which makes the room look comfortable and nice to be in, and lighting for use, which provides light for working, reading, and playing games.

Decor lighting should brighten the dark spots in a room. One satisfactory way of using this sort of lighting is to have a spotlamp shining into each corner, where light doesn't usually fall. Decor lighting shouldn't be gimmicky – no red bulbs, for instance – but just provide pools of light. Spotlamps can also be used to light up a picture or other object.

Lighting for use must be efficient, as all workspaces must be well lit. This includes kitchen working surfaces, desks and other worktops and places where people might be expected to sit and read or sew. It's just as important to have

good lighting by a child's play table or desk as in a living room or adult's workroom.

In a house where you are lucky enough to have good light coming through the windows, you should use this light for working if possible. Light for working should shine down onto the worktop without shining into the eyes of the worker and without casting a shadow over the area. Angled desk lamps are very good for this and particularly where the working position may change. In a kitchen, where the working position is more or less always the same, direct lights from the ceiling or spotlamps shining onto the chopping surface, cooker and sink will do a good job.

Bedside lamps should have this quality of good, directed light without shadow and should be chosen so that if the bed is shared one person's lamp will not disturb the other. After all, two people may not want to read at the same time.

Rise-and-fall lamps on a pulley are useful for dining, especially if you eat in the kitchen or living room. Any bright working lights can be switched off during the meal and the rise-and-fall pulled down to give a general, gentle light but not get in the way.

Dimmer switches are easy to have fixed and they are not expensive. They are useful in areas where you don't always want the same intensity of light; also for eating or for children's rooms, especially if a child is afraid of the dark. This is a useful way of lighting passages and staircases at night if you don't want to turn off the light completely.

You will find it helpful to have a light by a shaving mirror, by a dressing table, and inside deep cupboards (these can use a conventional switch or one that is fixed so that the door automatically switches on the light when opened).

Most lamps are designed to take a certain wattage of bulb – usually not more than 40w or 60w (the wattage is always marked on the lamp). Never put

Above: Opal styrene sphere on a rise-and-fall suspension unit provides a good light over a dining table. Global by Lumitron
Opposite, top: Adjustable spotlights in a choice of colours and sizes clip on the track. Lytesphere by Concord Lighting International
Opposite, bottom: Versatile, adjustable spot mounted on a clip fits onto anything up to 4cm thick. Clip spot by Habitat

in a stronger bulb than the lamp specifies; many expensive fittings have been ruined this way. When looking for lamps, check that the fitting is secure and that the bulb will fit into it easily.

Some chain stores are rightly admired for their practical, imaginative, modern and cheap lighting; there is every kind to choose from, including lighting track which is designed to take a row of lamps which slot into it. When buying track you should bear in mind that each make is slightly different and usually only that maker's lamps will fit into it. Some office equipment shops have excellent angled lamps, often cheaper than those found in department stores and specialist lighting shops.

Ordinary light bulbs give a yellowish light and it is necessary to choose lamp-shades carefully to achieve the right effect. Blues and greens give a rather cold light; red is warm but may look as though you're giving a permanent party unless it fits in with a lot of red decoration, and it certainly doesn't make a good working light. White gives a neutral-toned light, but a gold or yellow shade will look warmer and prettier.

It is actually cheaper to use fluorescent lighting than traditional tungsten filament bulbs. A fluorescent bulb will produce more than four times as much light as tungsten filament bulbs for the same amount of electricity. They last longer too, having a useful life of 5,000 hours or more (tungsten filament bulbs should last about 1,000 hours). Fluorescent bulbs are available in various sizes and colours have improved enormously; you should ask for a suitable colour for domestic use.

Now you have your basic, warm shell and you can move in. It doesn't matter if you have to sleep and eat on the floor; you have all you need to start off.

Furniture

Lots of factors will affect your choice of furniture: the size and style of your house; the size and shape of the rooms; your own taste; how much you can afford to spend and so on.

On the whole people are inclined to have too much furniture. It is best to start with the bare minimum and to add later when you will have had time to think about what you really need and how the rooms should be arranged. If the rooms are small they will almost certainly look their best and be easier to use with very little furniture indeed, unless you have a flair for collecting and arranging Victoriana and bits and pieces and like living in a junk shop atmosphere. (This is not meant to put you off – many people do, and manage to create an extraordinarily pleasing and extremely personal environment, but you must be confident and positive if you want to do it successfully.)

Stick to your own taste. If you have inherited some period furniture, it may suggest that the room should be furnished in a fairly traditional way. But if you are careful with colour and shape, and

This large kitchen/dining room contains a particularly well chosen selection of stripped pine country furniture.

especially if you have a strong personal taste in these things, furniture from different periods can be combined quite satisfactorily. New and old can live together happily if the dimensions and quality of design and manufacture are good. A carved Irish dresser need not be out of place with an old oak table and modern cane-backed chair. However, if the furniture is really not what you like or want, sell it. There's no point in having a 'dead' room; that's the old front parlour syndrome and a waste of space.

Rooms can be arranged in various ways and your choice of furniture may depend on whether you want to make the room face outwards, making the best of a good view; inwards, towards some worthwhile feature; or give the room several small centres instead of just one.

For some households, cushions or a low divan may be more comfortable, practical and inviting than a formal suite of chairs. Unless you have a very strong leaning towards some specific style of furniture, choose what is best for your life and likes at the moment. Your own tastes will automatically produce some sort of unity.

It is useful to have some idea of what furniture is available so that you can eliminate the unsuitable before you decide on the type that is right for you and your home.

Antique furniture, by definition, must be over 100 years old. It may be hideous, but equally you may find simple pieces that have the patina of age. A very few pieces, particularly chairs and dressers, go back to the Plantagenets. Heavy, carved Elizabethan and Jacobean oak is very fine. The style of furniture became lighter towards the end of the 17th century. The walnut furniture of the early years of the 18th century was most elegant, with its carved legs and secret drawers. Mahogany was readily available in this country by 1725, and in Georgian

times it replaced walnut for cabinet making. There were elaborate chairs, stools and two-seater sofas, and ornate writing and dressing tables and candelabra. Throughout the latter part of the 18th century furniture designs became more elegant and delicate, culminating in the attractive Sheraton styles with their thin, spindly legs and simple decoration. Furniture in the 1800s was extravagant, with scrolls and gilt figures, often Egyptian in detail, revolving bookcases, lions' legs and painted wood. The Victorians brought their own style of extravagance, with lots of plush and heavy decoration.

Antique furniture is now much sought after and extremely expensive, to be coveted rather than acquired, except by the very rich or the very dedicated. The same applies to the work of the best designers from our own century, Ambrose Heal, Gordon Russell, Ernest Race, John Makepeace, to name but four, whose simple, beautifully constructed pieces of furniture have already become collectors' items.

Old or junk furniture need not be as dilapidated as its name suggests. Although it cannot technically be termed 'antique', popular furniture made during the first half of this century is often soundly constructed, while the simplicity of its design makes it suitable for almost any house style. It is becoming more difficult to find good second-hand furniture, but it is still possible to find well made and well proportioned chests of drawers, tables and kitchen chairs. However, beware of cheap veneer, warped wood and worm.

Reproduction furniture is literally a copy of antique furniture, made using the same skills of manufacture. The only difference is that it is made now and not then and is often artificially 'aged'. The best of such furniture looks just like the real thing and is nearly as expensive.

Modern furniture uses the techniques and materials of our age. Thus we have chromed tubular frames, legs and arms; glass table tops; plastics and glass fibre mouldings. Some modern furniture is quite enormously expensive, but not necessarily all.

Foam has become a very practical and popular furnishing material. It is often used for upholstery in conventional furniture and also on its own to make floor cushions; unit furniture (which can be added to ad infinitum); mattresses, sofas, sofa beds and so on. There are various qualities and types and the best furniture will incorporate more than one, giving softness and firmness where it's needed. Several mail order firms deal in this kind of furniture.

High Street furniture varies enormously, from extremely imaginative, reasonably priced and good looking pieces including modern conventional foam and pine – to the duller but worthy traditional designs, some of which are not particularly good looking but usually comfortable.

Knock down is the term for furniture which is packed flat in boxes and which you slot or screw together yourself when you get it home. Beware of some large High Street shops and mail order firms who sell this kind of furniture. It is often very cheap and therefore tempting, but the frustrations can be enormous since it is sometimes carelessly packed and you may find half the screws are missing or that there are four left legs. Cheap knock-down furniture may be made of chipboard with a laminated finish, often made to look like teak. If you are collecting it yourself from the warehouse or showroom, open the package if possible and check that everything is there.

Choosing furniture

Don't be vague when buying furniture; always measure. If you want something to fit into an alcove or between two kitchen appliances or next to a door, it's no good hoping it will be the right size; a few millimetres will decide whether the thing will actually fit into its allotted space or not.

It may be useful to make a floor plan of the room and cut pieces of paper to the same scale to represent the furniture and juggle about with them until you get a satisfactory result. Remember that it's not enough to fit the furniture into a space on the paper; there must also be enough room to use it. People still have to find room for their knees or to stick their feet out, or to open a drawer or cupboard door. Chairs must be manœuvrable; you can't tuck people away neatly like dining chairs.

Remember that huge furniture is not suitable for very small rooms, nor tall furniture for small people. Children will probably prefer to have everything at a low level so they can reach their own toys and clothes and put them away themselves. This is one of the good reasons for having adaptable shelving systems in a children's room. The shelves can, of course, be raised as the children grow older.

Probably the most useful rule for furniture and furnishings is to try and find pieces for a particular situation rather than buy things you like the look of and then try to live with them. It is nearly always better to be patient for the time being and live with, on and by orange boxes and other make-do furniture than to buy medium-priced, slightly shoddy things which will become shabby all too soon, yet which still eat into your precious savings.

It is really remarkable what you can do with fabric remnants, a good adhesive and a staple gun. This make-do-and-mend policy has the advantage that it gives you time to consider what you really do need, and indeed you may find you actually prefer an emptyish house with room to move to one filled with furniture, however beautiful.

The vital thing is to have adequate storage at all times, because it is essential for everything to have a proper home, especially if there is more than one person using it.

For small houses, particularly, dual-purpose furniture can solve a lot of problems. However, it must be flexible in its arrangement. You must have enough room to pull it out or unfold it or turn it round, or whatever is necessary for it to serve its dual function. Other examples are shelving systems which incorporate cupboards, shelves and other fitments; storage boxes used as seating (window seats for instance); and dual-purpose beds (see below). Whatever dual-purpose furniture you choose, it should practically always be simple in concept. Anything too clever and gimmicky will probably not function well.

This versatile foam unit seating will easily convert from chair to bed. Single, double and corner pieces available. From the Bedsit range by Adeptus

This solidly built pine bunk bed unit with slatted bases can be separated to make twin beds. Hand made by Stokecroft Arts

Beds

A bed is the one thing you should never try to buy on the cheap. A poor mattress will give you bad sleep and possibly aches and pains, and will need renewing long before a better quality one. A mattress should be at least 125mm deep, and deeper for heavy people. Good quality foam mattresses are suitable for children or visitors and the best quality ones are adequate for adults too, but interior sprung mattresses are the most satisfactory if you can afford them. All upholstered mattresses in this country are made to a standard of construction and cleanliness laid down by the British Standards Institution. Look for the BSI Kitemark when buying; 90 per cent of British firms conform to this standard.

An open-sprung mattress consists of wire frame, springs, insulating material and upholstery padding with ticking on the top; some have specially firm edges. A pocket-sprung mattress has coil springs, each enclosed in a pocket of calico in a honeycomb. They are more resilient, more comfortable and will wear better.

Generally speaking a firm bed is better for the health than a soft one. The base should be firm and strong. The only way to tell whether a bed is right for you is to lie on it. Notice if it springs back into shape when you get up. Bounce on it to make sure the springs don't squeak. Check that it will get into your house and up the stairs. People moving into new homes have had to abandon double beds because they wouldn't get up the stairs.

Dual-purpose beds can be very useful. For example, a low divan could take the place of a sofa in a living room. You might put it against a wall with cushions along the back, or right in the middle of the room leaving the walls free for storage. It can be used as seating during the day and as a bed at night, perhaps leaving another room free for work or children.

Another example is the sofa bed. Foam seating is versatile in this respect and can often serve three or more purposes, turning into several easy chairs, a three-seater sofa or a bed for visitors, depending on how you arrange it. Other variations include beds that fold up into enormous cushions; beds with drawers underneath; folding beds and stacking beds.

Chairs

Comfort must be the priority when buying chairs. If a chair is comfortable to sit in, supports the back in the right places, is the right height and depth, you will nearly always find that it looks good too. A chair that looks good without being comfortable is just not worth the money spent on it. Better to have humdrum wooden kitchen chairs than chrome and leather backbreakers.

As with buying beds, you should try out a chair in the shop, but not in a heavy overcoat. Sit on it not just for a quick minute, but for long enough and in various positions so that you really get the feel of it. Chairs for relaxing should be soft but firm. It's usually better to have a back of some sort and many people find chairs with arms more comfortable than those without.

For upright sitting, working and eating, a chair should support the thigh, so the seat shouldn't be too short, and support the back without digging into it. For eating, the chair height should correspond to the table height. It is usual for a dining chair to have a seat height of 420mm, in which case the table should be about 720mm high.

For working, whether at a desk or table or at a kitchen worktop, one of the best kinds of chair is a typist's chair which can be swivelled round to adjust its height. These chairs are designed to support the body in the best way and the height change is obviously useful: in the kitchen you need to be higher up to reach the sink than for chopping vegetables or rolling pastry, and at a desk you need to be higher up for typing than for writing. (Another solution is to have a slightly lower surface for pastry rolling or typing.)

Stools which can fit under a worktop or table are useful when space is at a premium; stacking and folding chairs are invaluable too; a bench may take up less room and be easier for people to get onto than chairs in a cramped space between table and wall. Foam on its own is usually cheap, fairly long lasting and available in hundreds of different variations. But there is nothing like properly sprung upholstery for comfort and long life.

Unless you are prepared to fit your sofas and chairs with loose covers, which will need to be cleaned fairly often, a dark upholstery material in wool, tweed or corduroy would be the most practical. With large pieces of furniture like sofas, take care to make sure the colour works well with the rest of the room and does not 'jump out'. Sofas with loose back, side and seat cushions should have zipped covers which can be removed for dry cleaning; in this case the rest of the frame will probably not need the same attention.

Below left: Tipster stacking chair with polished chrome or nylon coated frame has a tip-up seat. Made by Race Furniture Below: Typist's chair with sturdy five-star base has manual or gas action height adjustment. Made by Arenson International

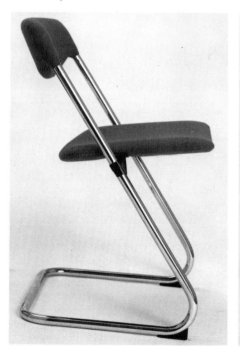
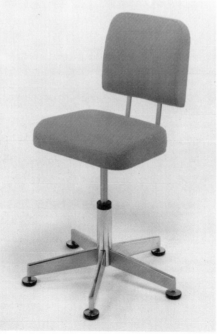

Tables

You will need one fairly sturdy table for eating. Other functions can be provided for by worktops or shelves, whether in the kitchen, workroom or elsewhere, but the dining table is important. Height is mentioned under chairs (see page 59); the actual size is important too. If you expect to be entertaining more than your immediate household it is obviously important to have an expanding table. There are various versions of expanding table, with drop flaps or extra leaves, most of which are expensive. But a circular table will take a surprising number of people.

If you have to use your kitchen for formal meals, even the humblest table will become a dining table if you put a cloth on it and dress it up a little. Remember that it should have no legs sticking out where people want to sit. Most modern tables have a polyurethane finish which makes them less vulnerable to heat and stains than polished tables, but a second-hand table may have been French polished, in which case you will have to take extra care with it. Pine is a popular wood for tables nowadays; it's simple and cheap and its pale colour is attractive with modern decorations. Solid wood is very difficult and expensive to come by now and many tables are finished in wood veneer.

In some way, that curious phenomenon the coffee table presents the most difficult design choice. Since it is very often placed in the middle of the room it needs to be an 'important' piece, but it is sometimes difficult to select exactly the right style. It should not be pretentious; nor too funny ha ha; nor so heavy that you cannot move it; nor with sharp edges for people to bark their shins on. Three very simple versions that serve their purpose admirably are shown on the opposite page. There are many variations on the theme and you will want to choose one that fits in with your furnishing style.

Where to look

There is an enormous choice of furniture but it is not always easy to know where to look or what to look for, especially if your local town has only one High Street furniture store full of teak and tassels. However, even in these uninviting little shops, there is quite often some nice furniture hidden away in the back, so it's always worth having a look. But rather than take the best of a bad lot simply because that's what's available immediately, try to get along to a largish town that has a choice of shops which sell a wider variety of well designed modern and period furniture.

Mail-order shopping is useful for people without a good choice of shops, especially those living in the depths of the country or a new town where the bus service may not be very good. Mail-order and cash-and-carry furniture is usually sold in 'knock-down' form (see page 57 for details).

Festo glass and aluminium coffee table (top) is sold in knock-down form.
Marcuso glass-topped coffee table (centre) has sturdy tubular metal legs.
Forrestal (bottom) is a similar style to the Marcuso, for those who prefer wood.
All these tables are made by Zanotta, and available from major furniture stores.

On the cheap

If you are very conscious of the need to produce decorations and furnishings for your home quickly and cheaply, so that you have at least one room which is smart, you can take some short cuts.

Indian cotton bedcovers with rings sewn on the back and fixed to a batten above a window can make a very attractive draw-up blind. In lieu of carpet, a pattern painted direct onto the floor with lino paint can be stunning. This technique was used years ago in the wooden houses in Scandinavia and a popular pattern was simulated black and white marble squares.

You can construct tables on practically any sort of support: large oil drums; the inevitable orange box; or a filing cabinet or old unpresentable piece of furniture with a circle of wood on top and covered up with a table cloth, as shown below. Don't despise the humble brick for table supports, shelf supports and book ends. A flush door, or even better a well veneered flush door, suitably sealed and supported on trestles, makes a perfect dining table.

If you're lucky enough to have some furniture given to you, don't despise it, even if it's not quite your thing. It is quite easy to make loose covers for chairs which will as often as not transform them. You can use mattress ticking (available from department stores) or a thin canvas or duck, or you can get quite hardy furnishing denim which is cheap as well.

If you haven't any furniture, you can easily make floor cushions using foam chips or expanded polystyrene granules. Foam blocks are available from some stores and market stalls; they can be cut to any size and thickness you want and covered with cheap cotton fabric. You can make up the covers and put in zips if you think you'll want to wash them.

Don't forget that auctions, discount lines, swap shops, jumble sales, junk shops, old bits and pieces from one's parents may all be useful sources for furniture and furnishings. The Salvation Army sometimes hold auctions of junk furniture at their depots (look in the telephone book). Local newspapers often have useful advertisements; local radio stations sometimes have swap programmes. The magazine *Exchange and Mart* can be useful if you get it early. Sometimes factories sell seconds and rejects cheaply. Discount stores and reject shops are useful sources of cheap goods, too.

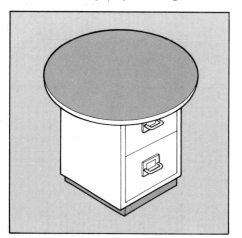

DRAWINGS BY CAROL PREEDY

Getting the work done

Who does the work?

Architect

Although you or your builder or even the man from the local council may be able to advise you on the very simplest conversion or extension – a square box over a garage, hidden from the road and the neighbours, for instance – anything more complicated should really have the benefit of an architect's experience and knowledge. An architect knows not only what materials will be suitable and available but also how to match the extension with the house, and he can deal with the planning regulations and so on as well. Try to choose an architect who specialises in house design and whose work you feel sympathetic towards. Find out what work he's done before either by talking to people who have used him or by asking him to show you photographs of his work.

A builder needs a drawing before he can build anything, and drawings are certainly required for the statutory authorities' approval. It is always advisable to contact an architect early on when you first think about your planned extension or conversion, rather than leave it to the last moment and expect drawings and consent to come through within a few weeks. Except for the very simplest structures this will just not be possible. You *can* bring someone in at the last minute, but don't expect his complete enthusiasm nor expect work to start tomorrow.

Building is a serious business and not to be undertaken lightly. If you do put up something that is later not approved you may have to tear it down. Many of the hard-luck stories one reads in the local papers are about people who have quite wilfully contravened the regulations. Information on which regulations are needed can be obtained from your local town hall.

Many people are a bit wary about approaching an architect, thinking that even a preliminary interview will involve them in high fees. This is just not true. But do ask at the outset what his charges are and he will explain them to you. He shouldn't charge you at all for just going to see him.

Many architects run a 'country doctor' practice where they are happy to help anyone who asks them; remember, it is rather flattering to be told 'I hear you are the best architect round here'. An architect will often produce a design for a fixed fee, and of course he will be able to deal with the local planning office, building inspector (for structural stability), public health officer (for drainage) and conduct party wall negotiations with your neighbour. For a fee of 12 per cent of the building cost most architects will design and supervise the construction as well as carrying out necessary negotiations for you.

The Royal Institute of British Architects operates a Client's Advisory Service from which you can get the names of three local architects chosen for their experience in the kind of work you want done. You can either write, telephone or visit them at their office in London (address on page 71), where they maintain comprehensive records of their members' work, supported in many cases by photographs. This service is free, and the RIBA suggests that you go and see all three architects before making up your mind. Alternatively, your library may have a directory of architects, and the council office may be able to help with a list of local architects.

Interior designer

An interior designer, as opposed to an architect, is often not trained in building design but may have acquired the necessary skill through practice. The better ones are well able to organise internal space and generally have the visual skill and imagination to make a room comfortable. However, the more limited ones are often only capable of helping you choose decorative finishes and may not understand the organisation of space and circulation patterns, which is such an important fundamental to any space design. This makes choosing a designer difficult.

If you don't know of any local designers, you can use the Designer Selection Service operated by the Design Council (address on page 71). For a fee they will give you a short-list of hand-picked designers in your area. The Society of Industrial Artists and Designers (address on page 71) will choose up to three suitable designers in your area from its list of members. There is no charge for this Design Information Service. Once you have chosen a designer, do insist on seeing examples of his work – if possible both in photographs and in reality.

If what you want is mainly help with fabrics, colour matching and so on, a good decorating shop may well be able to give you the advice you need. Alternatively, you could write to one of the home interest magazines that offer a colour scheme service.

Restoring a Victorian house to its original condition (as shown in these photographs) is as worth while as restoring an older house: Below: An opening cut in a structural wall – as here – must be supported by a steel or concrete beam built in to the satisfaction of the district surveyor. Right: The centre window has been removed from this bay and replaced by a pair of doors. All the architrave mouldings will be copied from the existing details. Below right: The staircase, dado and Lincrusta wallpaper have been replaced in the original style. Designer: Paul Winter

HOMER SYKES

Builder

Choosing a builder is even more difficult than choosing an architect or designer. Again, recommendation is the best and safest bet. Walk round the locality and see what houses are being worked on and read the builder's board outside. If there is no board, take care; the builder may be small or self employed, and he may be very good, but he could equally well be bad. He could also, of course, be cheaper than a large established building contractor. The advantage of going to a well established firm is that it will have a reputation to lose. And the amount of organisation and co-ordination between various building trades that you get with a bigger firm is possibly worth any higher management costs; they can also be kept to a completion date much more closely.

If you are employing an architect he will advise you to draw up a contract with your builder which for any work over, say, £10,000 should follow the standard RIBA form of contract. But if you insist on an exactly timed completion date, you should expect to pay the builder a little extra to cover the 'liquidated damages' clause which refers to completion dates.

If you are doing simple alterations and know exactly what you want and have the opportunity to engage a couple of self-employed men, no matter how friendly your negotiations with them, set down the terms of agreement with them in a letter beforehand so there will be no misunderstandings. It should cover the following details:

1 Their wages, hourly, daily or weekly.

2 That you will pay for building materials on receipt of invoices and, if they require it, a percentage on top of that – say $2\frac{1}{2}$ per cent for their having organised it for you.

3 The minimum period they will work for you, so that they won't disappear and leave you with an incomplete shell no-one else wants to finish.

4 Agreement as to working hours (say from 8am to 5pm with one hour's break for lunch, five days a week); this should ensure they arrive for work regularly rather than spasmodically.

These precautions may seem unnecessary, and between reasonable people may really be unnecessary, but where building work is concerned it is always better to reach firm prior agreement on these points because neither side can afford misunderstandings.

If you find someone whose work you think is good, make sure that he will actually come and do the work himself, and not subcontract it to someone else who may not work so well. If you have to live in the house while the work is going on, don't stand over the men and watch them all the time; this could be as upsetting for you as for them. But by all means inspect the work at the end of each day.

Aligning the various switches and controls on a wall gives a much tidier effect.

Estimates

Estimates are prepared against a detailed schedule called a specification of the work you want done. For instance, if all you want is a wall knocked down between two rooms, your specification should incorporate these points:

If the wall is load bearing, you will need to prop up the structure above with needling (a form of scaffolding). The wall below can then be cut away, and a beam put in (its size must be approved by the district surveyor or building surveyor in the country). If you are going to use a steel beam it should be cased with timber for fixing the plasterboard, then plastered. The skirtings and flooring must run continuously through both parts of the room. If you want doors between the two rooms you have to specify door linings, stops, the doors themselves, and hinges, bolts and handles.

Exactness at this early stage means you can have a precise cost, rather than one that creeps up towards completion because the builder says 'Oh, but I didn't include for that'.

On more complicated building work like adding a bathroom there may be various unknowns, such as special foundation requirements and position and depth of the drain, the cost of which remain unknown until excavations are actually made. For this purpose, while specifying exactly everything you do know (bath, taps, tiles, types of waste trap, source of hot water, lighting, ceiling finish, bath panels, showers and screens, mirrors and so on), it is sometimes necessary to include a provisional sum (PS) against the unknown item or items. This might be suggested by your builder, and when the work is actually carried out you must make sure that if he is operating alone you have daily work sheets and this provisional sum is offset.

On any contract over £3000 to £4000 it is prudent to allow a ten per cent contingency sum against any further unknowns. At least this will ensure you have the funds available. Remember that your estimate relates to a specific schedule of work. If you ask the builders to do any extra work (screw a mirror onto a wall or fix a cupboard, for instance) you should expect to pay for it.

For small jobs which are likely to start at once and not take longer than about three months, the builder should be asked to keep his prices firm and not to ask for increases due to fluctuations in labour and materials costs.

The advantage of having estimates before work starts is that if the work is likely to be more than you can afford, you can leave out certain items rather than have the anguish of starting something you can't afford to complete.

It is wise, unless the job is very small, to get three or four estimates, so that if two are similar and one much higher or lower you know there must be something wrong with it.

Order of work

If you are going to organise the work yourself without the benefit of advice from a building contracts manager, plan the order in a logical and systematic way. All electrical wiring and heating and gas installations, plumbing and drainage work should be done before any plastering is started. This applies to any basic interior insulation too. And all joinery work such as fitted cupboards, new doors, hatches, fitted furniture and other details should be completed before decorating. If you don't do things in the right order you may have to re-do work that is already completed, and this will involve you in extra cost and time.

Do leave ample time for plaster to dry out; about three months is needed in summer, and longer in winter. Any final decorations, whether paint or wallcoverings, applied while the plaster still holds some damp will peel and flake off.

If you are employing a building contractor it is the responsibility of the site foreman to see that his men work as efficiently as possible. But if you are employing direct labour the efficient planning of the operation is up to you.

Payments

Payments to a building contractor are usually made monthly. The amount payable should be certified by the architect on a standard form which shows the net retention (five per cent) until the end of the contract.

Once certified, the invoice should be paid within 14 days. It is important to make payments promptly to ensure a well disposed and viable builder, but if you don't employ an architect to make sure you are not paying for work not done and materials not delivered on site, you will have to keep a careful check and ask to see all the invoices and labour records. Self-employed men will probably want to be paid weekly; they may prefer to be paid in cash every Friday so you should arrange to have the cash ready.

Doing it yourself

Even if you are 'good with your hands' it is easy to underestimate the amount of time needed for a job. You may in the long run find it more satisfactory to call in professionals than to begin a long and complicated job which you can only work on at weekends.

On the whole it is wiser to avoid jobs such as alterations to walls, roofs or loft floors. Work on central heating, electrical and gas installations should be done by professionals.

Plastering is extremely difficult, messy and tiring. Dry rot and woodworm should be treated by professional specialists. However, laying floors, stripping paint, renewing woodwork, painting, wallpapering and so on can all save you money if you do them yourself. Don't start without a good and comprehensive tool kit. Don't try and save by buying poor quality materials. Always follow the instructions to the letter and when buying materials always over- rather than underestimate the amount you will need.

Addresses of manufacturers and retailers

Adeptus
9 Sicilian Avenue
Southampton Row
London WC1
01-405 5603
Retailer. Foam seating. Other branches.

Aeonics
92 Church Road
Mitcham
Surrey
01-640 1113
Manufacturer and retailer. Continental quilts. Mail order service.

Afia Carpets
81 Baker Street
London W1
01-935 0414
Retailer. Carpets. Good service.

Sally Anderson Ceramics
Parndon Mill
Elizabeth Way
Harlow
Essex
0279 20982
Designer and manufacturer. Ceramic wall and floor tiles.

Aram Designs
3 Kean Street
London WC2
01-240 3933
Retailer. Furniture, lighting.

Arrowtip
31-35 Stannary Street
London SE11
01-735 8848
Manufacturer and retailer. Polystyrene granules.

Laura Ashley
40 Sloane Street
London SW1
01-235 9728
Manufacturer and retailer. Wallpaper, fabrics. Mail order service.

Bedlam
114 Kensington Church Street
London W8
01-229 5341
Retailer. Beds, bedding, continental quilts.

Berger Paints
Freshwater Road
Dagenham
Essex
01-590 6030
Manufacturer. Helpful leaflets.

British Home Stores
129 Marylebone Road
London NW1
01-262 3288
Retailer. Lighting, bedlinen, accessories. Other branches.

Buyers and Sellers
120 Ladbroke Grove
London W10
01-229 1947
72 Uxbridge Road
London W12
01-743 4049
Retailer. Refrigerators, freezers, washing machines and dishwashers, slightly marked but in perfect working order and guaranteed. Prices 10 to 20% below discount houses.

Ceramic Consultants
The Old Brewery
Wish Ward
Rye
Sussex
07973 3038
Manufacturer and retailer. Ceramic wall and floor tiles. Rye pottery.
London showroom:
12 Connaught Street
London W2
01-723 7278

Coexistence
10 Argyle Street
Bath
Avon
0225 61507
Retailer. Furniture, fabrics, bathroom fittings, accessories. Interior design service.

Cole & Son
18 Mortimer Street
London W1
01-580 1066
Manufacturer and retailer. Paints, wallpapers, complementary fabrics.

Colour Counsellors
187 New Kings Road
London SW6
01-736 8326
Countrywide interior design service.

Concord Lighting International
241 City Road
London EC1
01-235 1200
Manufacturer. Large showroom. Advisory service.

CubeStore
58 Pembroke Road
London W8
01-602 2001
Manufacturer. Storage systems. Mail order service.

Cucina
4 Ladbroke Grove
London W11
01-229 1496
8 Englands Lane
Hampstead
London NW3
01-722 7093
Retailer. Furniture, accessories, china, glass. Mail order service.

Dalton Barton (Textiles)
2-4 Banbury Street
London E2
01-739 8444
Retailer. Textiles.

Elizabeth David
46 Bourne Street
London SW1
01-730 3123
Retailer. Cookware, kitchen utensils.
Mail order service on certain items.

Tempe Davies
107 Kentish Town Road
London NW1
01-485 1258
Retailer. Kitchen accessories, pine
furniture.

Designers Guild
277 Kings Road
London SW3
01-351 1271
Manufacturer and retailer.
Wallcoverings, fabrics, furniture,
accessories.

Divertimenti
68 Marylebone Lane
London W1
01-935 0689
Retailer. Cookware and tableware.

Felt and Hessian Shop
34 Greville Street
London EC1
01-405 6215
Retailer. Fabrics. Mail order service.

Focus Ceramics
213 Staines Road
Hounslow
Middlesex
01-570 6516
Importer, retailer. Ceramic wall and
floor tiles.

Mary Fox Linton
1 Elystan Street
London SW3
01-581 2188
Retailer. Complementary fabrics,
wallcoverings, carpets, tiles. Interior
design service.

Habitat
Hithercroft Road
Wallingford
Oxfordshire
0491 35000
Retailer. Furniture, fabrics, bedlinen,
accessories. Small charge for mail order
catalogue. Other branches.

Hamlet Furniture
Waverley Road
Beeches Industrial Estate
Yate
Bristol
Avon
0454 319090
Manufacturer. Pine furniture, Mail
order only from colour catalogue.

Heal's
196 Tottenham Court Road
London W1
01-636 1666
Retailer. Furniture, fabrics, kitchen
fittings, bedding, accessories.

David Hicks
101 Jermyn Street
London SW1
01-930 1991
Retailer. Furniture, fabrics, carpets,
accessories. Interior design service.

Knobs and Knockers
61-65 Judd Street
London WC1
01-387 0091
Retailer. Ironmongery, brass, china,
bathroom fittings.

Jotul Woodstoves
UK distributor: Simon Thorpe
New Road
Newcastle Emlyn
Dyfed
Wales
0239 710100
Norwegian wood-burning stoves, some
with hotplates, water heating kit available
on two models.

John Lewis
278/306 Oxford Street
London W1
01-629 7711
Retailer. Furniture, bedding, kitchen
and bathroom fittings, lighting,
accessories. Other branches.

Liden Products
Clothier House
Trading Estate
Hamm Moore Lane
Addlestone
Surrey
Weybridge 53355
Manufacturer. Whitewood furniture.
Mail order service.

Limericks Linens
Hamlet Court Road
Westcliffe on Sea
Essex
0702 43486
Retailer. Linen and sheeting. Mail
order service.

MacCulloch and Wallis
25 Dering Street
London W1
01-629 0311
Retailer. Fabrics, haberdashery. Mail
order service.

Master Tiler
31 Dover Street
London W1
01-493 4174
Retailer. Ceramic wall and floor tiles.

David Mellor
4 Sloane Square
London SW1
01-730 4259
Manufacturer and retailer. Cookware and kitchen accessories. Mail order service.

Merchant Chandler
72 New Kings Road
London SW6
01-736 6141
Retailer. China, glass, kitchen accessories, furniture.

Mothercare
Cherry Tree Road
Watford
Hertfordshire
92 33577
Retailer. Children's furniture. Mail order service. Other branches.

New Dimension
Manor Road
West Ealing
London W13
01-998 2900
Retailer. Furniture, kitchen units, accessories. Other branches.

John Oliver
33 Pembridge Road
London W11
01-727 3735
Manufacturer and retailer. Paints, co-ordinating wallpapers and fabrics. Mail order service.

Osborne & Little
304 Kings Road
London SW3
01-352 1456
Manufacturer and retailer. Wallpapers, fabrics.

Oscar Woollens
421 Finchley Road
London NW3
01-435 7750
Retailer. Furniture, carpets.

Porcupine Furniture
Beaumont Road
Banbury
Oxfordshire
0295 51721
Manufacturer and retailer. Solid pine kitchen units, furniture.

Queensway Discount Warehouses
Norfolk Tower
Surrey Street
Norwich
0603 60277
Retailer. Furniture, kitchen units, carpets. Other branches.

The Reject Shop
245 Brompton Road
London SW3
01-584 7611
209 Tottenham Court Road
London W1
01-580 2895
Retailer. Perfect, imperfect and discontinued china, glass and accessories. Branches in Brighton, Kingston, Watford.

Rooksmoor Mills
Bath Road
Near Stroud
Gloucestershire
045 387 2577
Retailer. Furniture, floorcoverings. Mail order service.

Rye Pottery
77 Ferry Road
Rye
Sussex
07973 3363
Manufacturer and retailer. Pottery.

Sapphire Carpets and Furniture Centre
18-24 Bond Street
London W5
01-579 2323
Retailer. Carpets, bedding, furniture.

Skye Ceramics
240 Brompton Road
London SW3
01-584 9818
Manufacturer and retailer. Ceramic wall and floor tiles.

Stokecroft Arts
92-94 Caledonian Road
London N1
01-278 6874
107-109 Hammersmith Road
London W14
01-603 8138
Manufacturer and retailer. Hand-made pine furniture. Mail order service.

The Tile Mart
151 Great Portland Street
London W1
01-580 3814
Retailer. Ceramic tiles. Other branches.

UBM (United Builders' Merchants)
Avon Works
Winterstoke Road
Bristol
0272 664611
Retailer. Kitchen and bathroom fittings. Other branches.

Wicanders (Great Britain)
Showroom:
41 Berners Street
London W1
01-636 5959
Manufacturer. Cork wall and floor tiles. Mail order service.

Addresses of advice sources

Building Centre
26 Store Street
London WC1
01-637 9001
Advice on manufacturers and materials;
heating advice; bookshop.

Consumers' Association
14 Buckingham Street
London WC2
01-839 1222

Cuprinol
Adderwell
Frome
Somerset
0373 5151
Wood preservation.

Design Council
The Design Centre
28 Haymarket
London SW1
01-839 8000
Designer Selection Service; Design
Index; bookshop.

Design Council Scottish Committee
The Scottish Design Centre
72 St Vincent Street
Glasgow 2
041-221 6121

Electricity and gas services
These are organised locally and details
can be found in local telephone
directories.

Electrical Contractors' Association
ESCA House
32-34 Palace Court
London W2
01-229 1266

Heating and Ventilating Contractors'
Association
ESCA House
32-34 Palace Court
London W2
01-229 2488

HMSO Bookshop
PO Box 569
London SE1
01-928 1321

National Association of Plumbing,
Heating and Mechanical Services
Contractors
6 Gate Street
London WC2
01-405 2678

National House Building Council
58 Portland Place
London W1
01-387 7201

Office of Fair Trading
Field House
Bream's Buildings
London EC4
01-242 2858

Royal Institute of British Architects
66 Portland Place
London W1
01-580 5533
Client's Advisory Service.

RIBA Regional Offices
See local telephone directory
for addresses.

Society of Industrial Artists and
Designers
12 Carlton House Terrace
01-930 1911
Design Information Service.

Yellow Pages
Addresses of local plumbers, builders,
electrical contractors, builders'
merchants etc.

Further reading

Book of Home Improvements
Reader's Digest Association, 1976

Cheap Chic
Caterine Milinaire and Carol Troy
Omnibus Press, 1976

Choosing your Central Heating
Hamlyn Publishing Group, 1974

Electricity Supply and Safety
Ed Edith Rudinger
Consumers' Association, 1972

Flat Broke
Barbara Chandler
Pitman Publishing, 1976

Good Housekeeping Kitchens
Diana Austen and Catherine Davies
Ebury Press, 1976

The House Book
Terence Conran
Mitchell Beazley, 1974

Interior Decorating made Simple
Barty Phillips
Aldus Books, 1974

Keeping Warm for Half the Cost
J A Colesby and P J Townsend
Prism Press, 1976

The Legal Side of Buying a House
Ed Edith Rudinger
Consumers' Association, 1974

Living for Today
Karen Fisher
Thames and Hudson, 1973

The Pauper's Homemaking Book
Jocasta Innes
Penguin Books, 1976

Reader's Digest Household Manual
Reader's Digest Association, 1977

Wonderworker
Barty Phillips
Sidgwick and Jackson, 1977